A Mechanic's Code

by

Jason Sparrow

Dedicated to my wife Jessica and

my daughter Jade.

Love you two, always!

Jason

These strategies, when combined, can significantly reduce the risk of falling victim to hackers and help you maintain a higher level of online security.

1. Use Strong, Unique Passwords
    - Use complex passwords that include upper and lowercase letters, numbers, and symbols. Avoid reusing passwords across multiple sites.
    - Consider using a password manager to generate and store strong passwords securely.
2. Enable Two-Factor Authentication (2FA)
    - Add an extra layer of security to your accounts by enabling 2FA, which requires you to enter a secondary code (usually sent to your phone) in addition to your password.
3. Keep Software Updated
    - Regularly update your operating system, applications, and antivirus software to protect against the latest security vulnerabilities.
    - Enable automatic updates whenever possible to stay current.
4. Be Wary of Phishing Attempts
    - Be cautious about unsolicited emails or messages asking for sensitive information. Hackers often disguise themselves as legitimate organizations to steal your data.
    - Double-check email addresses and URLs before clicking on links or downloading attachments.
5. Use a VPN on Public Wi-Fi
    - When accessing the internet through public Wi-Fi (e.g., cafes, airports), use a Virtual Private Network

(VPN) to encrypt your connection and keep your data safe from hackers.

6. Secure Your Home Wi-Fi Network
- Change the default password on your router and use WPA3 or WPA2 encryption to protect your network.
- Turn off features like remote management and make sure your router firmware is up to date.

7. Install Antivirus and Anti-Malware Software
- Use reputable antivirus and anti-malware programs to detect and prevent malicious software from infecting your devices.
- Regularly scan your devices for potential threats.

8. Limit Personal Information Sharing
- Avoid sharing excessive personal information on social media or online forums, as hackers can use this data for targeted attacks or identity theft.
- Adjust privacy settings on your social media accounts to control who can see your posts.

9. Use Encrypted Communication
- For sensitive communications, use encrypted messaging apps like Signal or WhatsApp.
- If sending important files, ensure they are encrypted before transmission.

10. Back Up Your Data Regularly
- Keep regular backups of important files on external drives or in cloud storage. If your data is compromised by malware or ransomware, having backups will allow you to recover your information without paying a ransom.

Foreword

As technology continues to advance and become deeply embedded in our everyday lives, the need for cybersecurity has never been more critical. With nearly every aspect of modern life connected to the digital world be it banking, communication, or personal data storage the stakes are high. A single vulnerability can lead to dire consequences, not only for individuals but also for entire organizations and governments.

This book stems from both my academic journey as a cybersecurity student and my deep curiosity about the digital threats that affect us all. When I began studying cybersecurity, I quickly realized that it wasn't just about defending systems from hackers; it was about understanding the evolving landscape of cybercrime, anticipating threats, and developing strategies to counteract them before they even arise.

Throughout this book, I aim to not only highlight key issues in cybersecurity but also to challenge readers to think critically about the solutions. As a lifelong student in this field, I hope to inspire others whether seasoned professionals, students, or those simply concerned about their online safety to become more aware and proactive about their digital security.

I dedicate this work to my family, whose unwavering support has been a constant source of motivation. To my wife, my daughter, and even our dog, thank you for being there through the long nights and countless hours spent learning and writing. Without your patience and encouragement, this project wouldn't have been possible.

Lastly, I hope this book serves as a useful resource and sparks new discussions around the importance of cybersecurity in our fast-paced digital world.

Jason Sparrow
Lifelong Cybersecurity Student

Chapter 1 - Sentinel's Gambit

In the bustling heart of Silverfield, nestled within the urban sprawl, lies the unassuming facade of Phoenix Aviation, a civilian aviation firm with a secret dual identity. Beyond its polished exterior, Phoenix Aviation serves as a covert military weapons manufacturer, its operations shrouded in secrecy and its influence extending far beyond the boundaries of its outward civilian role.

Though its outward identity projects the polished image of a civilian aviation firm, Phoenix Aviation operates with the secrecy and precision of a clandestine government agency. The few who know its true nature understand that its reach extends far beyond the hangars and offices that comprise its visible footprint. Behind reinforced walls and biometric locks, research teams develop advanced weaponry and surveillance technologies for covert military operations. Each employee within this hidden sector is bound by layers of confidentiality agreements and non-disclosure contracts, while security protocols are so stringent that breaches are almost unheard of. Even so, Phoenix Aviation's covert activities are veiled by layers of misdirection, with public records tightly controlled and financial documents that tell only part of the story. For Phoenix, secrecy is more than a necessity; it is a matter of survival.

Phoenix Aviation's role in Silverfield goes beyond that of a typical corporation. It is woven into the fabric of the city itself, funding public initiatives, supporting local infrastructure, and providing employment for thousands. Its influence is so vast that the company has become a de facto governing entity, shaping policies and decisions in ways that directly benefit its dual identity. When Phoenix expands or shifts operations, it impacts the city's economy, its daily rhythms, and even its skyline. City officials often defer to Phoenix executives on matters of development, public works, and security, as the company's interests and the city's well-being have become inextricably linked. The citizens, knowingly or unknowingly, rely on Phoenix not only for jobs but for stability, safety, and a semblance of order making Phoenix Aviation as much a part of Silverfield's foundation as any elected government.

On a seemingly ordinary day, with the sun casting its golden glow over the cityscape, the hum of business as usual permeates the corridors of Phoenix Aviation. Employees scurry about their tasks, the air filled with the low murmur of conversation and the occasional ring of telephones.

But beneath this show of normalcy, a storm brews in the digital realm.Little did the employees know, a malicious force lurks in the shadows of cyberspace, determined to unleash chaos upon the unsuspecting company.

It begins with a subtle ripple, a spike in data traffic, that soon escalates into a torrential flood, overwhelming Phoenix Aviation's servers in a relentless Distributed Denial of Service (DDoS) assault. The attack's potential for widespread disruption looms large, as Phoenix's systems support key city operations. If the situation worsens, grounded flights, flickering traffic lights, and stalled financial transactions could grind Silverfield to a pause, exposing the city's dependence on Phoenix's infrastructure.

The streets of Silverfield buzz with an uneasy calm, as rumors of disruptions spread. Concerned drivers glance at traffic lights that momentarily lag, and nervous commuters watch delayed flight schedules flash across airport monitors. The city seems to hold its breath, teetering on the edge of chaos, its reliance on Phoenix Aviation's stability becoming glaringly evident.

In the command room of Phoenix Aviation, a sense of urgency hangs heavy in the air as the higher-ups scramble to regain control. Frantic fingers fly across keyboards, panicked voices echo off the walls, and sweat beads on furrowed brows as the team races against the clock to stem the tide of digital intrusion.

Amidst the chaos, a lone figure stands out. Randon. A seasoned veteran of the digital battlefield. His steely gaze fixed on the flickering screens before him. With a sense of determination born of years of experience, he navigates the maze-like depths of Phoenix Aviation's network, seeking out the source of the relentless assault.

As the minutes tick by and seconds get faster each second with less and less time to spare, Randon's efforts pay off. With a flick of his wrist and a final keystroke, he initiates a protocol designed to isolate the company's servers from the outside world, erecting a digital barrier in a last-ditch attempt to safeguard their systems. With one click, all of this could be over, and they'd all return to their normal work to prevent a situation like this from happening again.

How could they have been so stupid, Randon thought to himself. *To let something like this even get close to happening?*

But fate, it seems, has other plans. In the blink of an eye, the lights flicker and die, plunging the command room into darkness. Panic grips the room as the backup generators roar to life, especially Randon, casting a sickly glow over the faces of the assembled employees.

"It's impossible." One of the employees says, completely stunned. "This has never happened before!" Randon could hear the panic in the employees voice. But Randon knows something is coming after.

"Wait…" Randon says to the employees, as the lights flicker back on, the hum of backup generators fills the room, and a single terminal flickers to life amidst the darkness. The usual Phoenix Aviation command prompt begins to boot, its familiar structure scrolling by: system diagnostics, kernel loading, network configurations. But as the boot sequence finishes, something is wrong.

Instead of the expected $phoenixav prompt, the screen settles on a stark and unsettling line:

[sentinel@phoenixav /]$
[sentinel@phoenixav /]$
[sentinel@phoenixav /]$ I am Sentinel. I have taken your system by force. I will return it to you unharmed for a 1 time payment of 10 million dollars. Until then, I will be copying all of your files and making what changes I want. You'll see I am NOT to be messed with. I will make contact soon to tell you how to pay. I will now begin to run my codes. DO NOT INTERFERE!

The cursor flashes menacingly, almost taunting the stunned employees. Then, one by one, commands begin appearing as if typed by an unseen hand, each executed with precision. Files list, permissions alterations, and secure directories unlock, all unfolding in real time. The screen becomes a symphony of controlled chaos as Sentinel's presence makes itself known, not as a rogue process, but as the system's new master.

Randon stares at the screen, the gravity of the situation sinking in. "They're not just in," he mutters under his breath. "They've taken root!"

The team watches in paralyzed silence as Sentinel's control deepens, their demands and actions scrawling across the display like a digital manifesto. For Randon and his team, the battle is no longer just to stop the attack, it's to reclaim their own system from an adversary who knows it better than they do.

With each passing moment, Sentinel's grip tightens, their control growing more solid. The employees of Phoenix Aviation are left reeling, their world turned upside down by a foe they cannot see and cannot comprehend. Randon tries not to follow and instead be a leader, but with this kind of enemy that cannot be seen, it's hard for him to maintain his balance.

In the dim glow of backup lights, Randon stands by the central console, his gaze darting between screens. Bill, the lead network engineer, wipes his brow, tension visible in his every movement and every muscle Around them, a few other team members hover, eyes fixed on their monitors.

"Alright, Bill," says Randon in a tense tone, "this is your operation. What exactly are we dealing with here?"

"It's ugly," Bill replies, his face grim. "The DDoS hit us hard. It's not just volume; they're targeting specific public-facing servers. Our monitoring tools are overwhelmed; they're taking down everything we'd usually rely on to respond fast. We really need to get in contact and pay this ransom. Phoenix has the reserves"

Randon nods, his eyes narrowing as he processes the information. "Classic distraction move. But this isn't just an attack; they've just taken the king. The real game starts now. There will be no need to pay this 2 bit hacker. I've got his number. I was trained for this."

His eyes stay fixed on the monitor as he barks orders. "Karen, cross-reference any SHA-256 hash anomalies with yesterday's process logs, then pipe that into the SIEM to filter out false positives. And reroute flagged IPs to our honeypot."

Karen stares blankly, her brow furrows. "Um...SHA what?"

Randon softens his tone. "Just look for anything unusual in the access logs from yesterday. Anything that doesn't belong, tag it for me."

Karen nods, smiling faintly with eyes glistening with confusion and possible fear for the company. "Got it, sir. Thanks for the translation."

"You're doing great," Randon says with a quick nod of encouragement.

Karen returns to her task, more confident now. Meanwhile, Randon scans the logs. "They're hitting us hard from the outside, flooding public-facing systems and burying our response capabilities."

Karen, pausing her work, looks up from her glowing computer. "Sir, if it's just a DDoS, shouldn't our critical systems be safe? We've segmented the public network from the core."

Randon turns to her, his expression serious. "Good thinking, Karen. But they've hit us where it hurts. The attack's flooding our external firewalls and tying up our response systems, making it easier for them to slip through undetected." He shifts his focus to Bill. "Bill, do we have any intel on what their game plan is here?"

Bill grimaces. "They're running a network scan. We're seeing targeted queries for high-value assets, classified documents, credential stores, anything with elevated access permissions. They're systematically sweeping through shared drives and mapped resources. I'll start looking for escalation points. I've got that area covered."

"Classic," Randon says, his tone dark. "The DDoS is their cover while they hunt for the crown jewels. What about power? Why did the UPS fail?"

Mike, the systems operator, shifts nervously in his seat. "The power cut was…strange. Our backup generators kicked in, but the brief interruption threw off our primary defenses. It takes a few seconds to switch systems over, and that must've been enough for them to push through. It's like they knew our setup better than we do."

Randon scowled, frustration written across his face. "Of course. They're exploiting every gap. Alright, here's what we need: Bill, I want you to focus on isolating that escalation point. Karen, scan every log for recent access points and anything that looks out of place. Mike, run diagnostics on the backup systems. I want to know how they're sneaking through."

Bill hesitates for a moment, then says, "Randon...there's something else. If Sentinel is using a Metasploit-type framework, this isn't amateur work. Whoever's behind this knows exactly how to maneuver inside our network. It's like they've studied our defenses."

"That's my worry," Randon says grimly. "This is more than just an attack; it's a full-blown infiltration. We're playing catch-up in our own system."

"And we're still dealing with the DDoS on top of all that," Karen adds, her voice heavy with frustration. "It's not just a distraction; it's slowing us down at every turn."

Randon exhales sharply. "Alright, everyone, let's dig in. We're going to have to outsmart them in our own backyard. This isn't just about stopping the attack now; we need to figure out how they're staying a step ahead. They know more about our setup than anyone should."

Later, as the room buzzes with activity, Karen approaches Randon quietly, her voice low. "Sir, I didn't want to say this in front of everyone, but...well, you said if there was anything unusual to let you know. Well there's something strange in the logs. A manual override command was issued just before the power cut. It wasn't automated."

Randon's expression hardens, and he nods slowly. "You're saying someone inside triggered it?"

Karen hesitates, then nods. "It looks that way."

Randon glances around the room, his voice dropping further. "Keep this between us for now. If we have an insider, they've already done enough damage."

The team exchanges tense looks, bracing themselves for the storm ahead. Though Randon remains steadfast, his mind racing as he formulates a plan to counter Sentinel's calculated assault. The hum of backup systems and the flicker of monitors create a charged atmosphere, each team member silently grappling with the enormity of the battle unfolding in their own network.

The sharp ring of the red phone cuts through the dimly lit room, freezing everyone in place. The big boss hesitates, his hand hovering near the receiver as though reluctant to take the call. But Randon steps forward, his resolve unshaken, and picks up the phone.

A cold, detached voice greets him. "They're sending in NexTech."

Randon's jaw tightens as the name reverberates through the room. Karen immediately lets out a low groan dreading what's to come. "NexTech? Great. That's just what we need."

"They're glorified janitors," Mike mutters, rolling his eyes. "They show up late, slap on some overpriced software, and pretend they fixed everything."

"They've botched half the breaches they've been called in for," Karen adds. "If this is our big backup, we're screwed."

Bill, however, slams his fist on the desk, his voice rising above the murmurs. "Enough! Say what you want, but NexTech has handled bigger disasters than YOU ever will. You think they're perfect? No one is, but they've pulled companies back from the brink time and time again. While you're busy sneering, they might be the only reason we don't lose everything tonight. So how about showing some respect and letting them do their job? "

Randon's gaze remains fixed on the terminal, his thoughts racing. He doesn't join the argument continuing in the background; he doesn't have to. Suspicion gnaws at the edges of his mind. Whether NexTech is here to help or simply to report back to Phoenix's higher-ups, their presence doesn't sit right. If Sentinel knows Phoenix's setup as well as he seems to, would NexTech's involvement tip the scales or just create more vulnerabilities?

Lost in his thoughts and a racing heart, Randon makes a decision. If Phoenix is calling in reinforcements, then so would he. His fingers hover over the keys as the thought sharpens into a plan. He knows exactly who to call.

Chapter 2 - A call to action

As the sun dipped below the horizon, casting long shadows across the deserted streets of Silverfield, Jason found himself engrossed in his workshop, the steady hum of machinery providing a soothing backdrop to his work. With nimble fingers, he delicately soldered components to a printed circuit board, his mind focused on the task at hand.

"I can't believe I went so far out of tuning parameters that I actually blew a capacitor, but at least it didn't put a hole in a piston!" he mused to himself, a wry grin playing at the corners of his lips. "That just means we need more work!"

Setting down his soldering iron with a satisfied sigh, Jason's attention was drawn to a soft chime from his computer. A new email notification blinked in the corner of the screen. Clicking it open, he scanned the cryptic message:

Subject: Only You Can Fix This
Jason,
Your work is known far beyond the workshops of Silverfield. I have a problem that only someone with your precision and ingenuity can solve. We have a serious cybersecurity incident, and I think you are more connected than you know.
This isn't a job, it's a necessity. Meet me at Phoenix Aviation by **midnight**. No tools. No distractions. Just you. There's no time to waste.
        -A Professional

Jason frowned, about to reread the email, but the screen abruptly shifted to diagnostic readouts from the Supra's ECU. The flood of data demanded his attention, and the strange message was pushed to the back of his mind. For now.

With a quick glance at the screen, Jason's eyes widened in surprise as he realized that the electronic control unit (ECU) of his latest project, a sleek 1985 turbocharged Supra, was back online and ready for another round of tinkering. Without missing a beat, he delved into his work analyzing the fuel map and began inputting new variables gleaned from a heavily annotated notebook that seemed to have been plucked straight from the mind of a mad scientist.

Hours passed as Jason had become engrossed in fine-tuning the ECU. It wasn't until the chime sounded again that he remembered the strange email from earlier. Another message popped up on the screen, drawing his curiosity back to the sender.

Subject: Seriously, Jason?
Jason,
I know you're probably too busy rebuilding Silverfields fastest car to check your inbox, but I'm serious. This is urgent.

Stop pretending you don't see these. Just get to Phoenix before **midnight**. Bring yourself and your brilliance and maybe leave the wrenches behind this time. This time I need you to remember that code and

Don't make me email again. Nobody likes a spammer.
  -Someone Who's Running Out of Patience

Jason let out a short breathy laugh, shaking his head. "What kind of prank is this? Fastest car in Silverfield? Yeah, right. I'm not even done fine-tuning the thing," he muttered. But his amusement quickly gave way to unease. The sender clearly knew something about him, but who? And why now?

Glancing at the time on his computer just past 10 PMJason leaned back in his chair, trying to shake off the nagging thought that maybe this wasn't just a joke. The work in front of him seemed less important now, but he couldn't bring himself to act on the emails. Not yet.

An hour slipped by, the Supra's diagnostics flickering in the corner of his screen as Jason tinkered absentmindedly. Just as he was about to pack it in for the night, the chime came again, more jarring this time. Jason sat upright as he read the latest message, his pulse quickening.

Subject: Midnight is the Deadline

Jason,

Silverfield doesn't need another problem and neither do you. This is bigger than you realize, and it's not just about what you can build or fix. It's about what you can stop. **If this breach isn't stopped, the fallout will spread beyond Silverfield. It's already in motion, and we can't hold the line much longer without you.**

Please, Jason. Show up at Phoenix by MIDNIGHT. I wouldn't ask if it wasn't critical.

You don't have to trust me. Just trust that this matters.

-A Believer

Jason glanced at the clock; 11:00 PM. The tone of this email was different, almost desperate. His unease solidified into something heavier, something he couldn't ignore. Midnight was less than an hour away, and curiosity had become an almost unbearable pull.

With a resigned sigh, Jason stood, grabbed his jacket, and headed for the door. "Alright, whoever you are, you've got my attention."

With a roar of an engine and a spray of gravel, Jason's customized Supra tore down the deserted streets of Silverfield. Its sleek form cuts through the darkness like a knife through butter. With each passing mile, his mind raced with questions, his curiosity growing by the tantalizing mystery that awaited him.

The 1985 turbocharged Supra, meticulously crafted and expertly customized by Jason, is a true marvel of automotive engineering. Boasting a plethora of performance-enhancing modifications, this iconic vehicle stands as a testament to Jason's unparalleled skill and dedication to his craft.

At the center of this beast lies a completely fabricated front-facing intake manifold, designed to optimize airflow and maximize power output. Paired with an extra-large intercooler, this setup ensures that the engine air charge remains cool under pressure, allowing for sustained performance even in the most demanding conditions.

Fuel delivery is handled with precision, thanks to the installation of 440 cc injectors and a 255 LPH fuel pump, ensuring ample fuel flow to feed the hungry engine. And with the MegaAssert ECU at the helm, equipped with expansion packs for added versatility, the Supra's engine management system is nothing short of state-of-the-art.

But it's not just under the hood where Jason's expertise shines. The Supra's drivetrain has been carefully fine-tuned for maximum efficiency and responsiveness. With full sequential ignition and injection systems, as well as custom-made camshaft and crankshaft position sensors, every aspect of the engine's operation has been optimized for peak performance.

Inside the cockpit, the Supra is a sight to behold, with a digital dash display and information gauges providing real-time feedback on vital engine parameters. And with data logging capabilities built-in, Jason has ensured that every aspect of the Supra's performance can be monitored and analyzed with precision.

But perhaps most impressive of all is the fact that Jason wrote the entire repair manual for this custom masterpiece, a testament to his deep understanding of the vehicle and its intricacies. The 1985 Celica Supra customized by Jason is more than just a car. It's a testament to the power of passion, ingenuity, and expertise.

As Jason sped down the empty streets, he hit the button to call Shane, a longtime friend and fellow gearhead who knew every trick in the book when it came to fixing cars.

"Hey, Shane," Jason said, leaning against his workbench. "Quick questionI blew out a capacitor earlier. You ever had one pop on you in a DIY setup?"

Shane laughed on the other end of the line. "Yeah, only every other time I tweak something. Bet you cranked up the voltage without dialing back the fuel trim first, right?"

Jason chuckled, shaking his head. "Yeah, that's pretty much it. I was sure I'd mapped it right, but it threw everything off."

There was a brief pause before Shane's tone shifted, curiosity creeping in. "So, I can hear the car in the background. Where are you headed, anyway? It's gotta be late."

Jason started to answer but hesitated, his mind flicking to the cryptic emails and the strange sense of urgency they brought. How was he supposed to explain this to Shane; someone who didn't care about cybersecurity, codes, or breaches?

"It's… complicated," Jason finally said, keeping his tone light. "Just a weird thing I have to check out. Not really sure what it's all about myself, honestly."

"Right," Shane said with a chuckle. "Well, try not to blow anything else up while you're at it."

Jason laughed, as he hung up, but his mind drifted back to the email and the strange sense of urgency behind it. He wasn't an expert in tone, but he knew something was up with that email. And he was going to find out what.

The headquarters of Phoenix Aviation loomed before him, a towering monolith of glass and steel that reflected the dim city lights. Jason had grown up near this facility, passing it countless times without ever paying it much attention, yet he'd never once been inside. Now, standing in its shadow, he felt a strange, almost unsettling pull as he took in its sharp, unyielding architecture. The exterior was sleek, cold, and impersonal, with reflective windows that gave nothing away.

Arriving at the meeting with minutes to spare, Jason was met by a group of NexTech associates who wasted no time in ushering him inside. "Why am I here?" he tried to ask, but his questions fell on deaf ears as the associates hustled him through the labyrinthine corridors of the sprawling complex.

Inside, the halls stretched on like a maze, dimly lit and lined with reinforced doors, each leading to spaces he could only imagine. The command room was a fortress of screens and high-tech consoles, their glow casting a pale light across the faces of Phoenix employees, all working in tense silence. The atmosphere felt heavy, almost claustrophobic, filled with the hum of machinery and the soft, constant beeping of alerts. Jason couldn't shake the feeling that this place was more than just a corporate office; it felt like the nerve center of something larger, something hidden beneath layers of secrecy.

As they reached the office in the back of the command room, Jason's curiosity reached a fever pitch, his mind buzzing with anticipation. But before he could voice his questions, the door swung open, revealing a figure that sent a chill down his spine. A figure he recognized all too well.

"Randon," he whispered, his voice barely a breath as the pieces of the puzzle fell into place. And with a sinking feeling in the pit of his stomach, Jason realized that he was about to embark on the journey of a lifetime.

Chapter 3 - Navigating the Unknown

The command room buzzed with activity as Jason entered the unfamiliar world of cybersecurity. . Surrounded by a team of experts, he couldn't shake the feeling of being out of his depth. But as Randon guided him through the intricacies of digital defense, Jason's intuition began to kick in, his mind racing to grasp the complexities of the task at hand.

"Alright, let's go over the playbook." Randon declared, his voice cutting through the tension like a knife. With a sense of purpose, the team gathered around the central terminal, their eyes fixed on the screen as Randon outlined their strategy for countering Sentinel's cyber onslaught.

As they reviewed the plan, Jason's mind whirred with possibilities. Drawing upon his experience with automotive electronics, he began to focus on parallels between the intricacies of digital systems and the inner workings of the machines he knew so well. With each passing moment, his confidence grew, his mind ablaze with newfound understanding.

Jason shifted uneasily, watching the lines of code scroll by. He might not know the specifics of security, but he was no stranger to digital systems and had spent countless hours tweaking, troubleshooting, and even building computer setups in his garage.

But amidst the flurry of activity, He couldn't shake the feeling of unease that gnawed at his gut. Why had he been chosen for this task? What connection did he have to Sentinel, the mysterious cybercriminal wreaking havoc upon Phoenix Aviation?

Determined to find answers, Jason seized a momentary lull in the pending proceedings to approach Randon, their footsteps echoing off the cold, sterile walls of the command room. With a touch of exhaustion Randon sank into a nearby chair, his gaze fixed on the floor as he wrestled with his thoughts. Jason took a seat next to Randon, to get his attention.

"So, Jason, how's the shop going? I've heard you're making some serious waves in the automotive world" Randon awkwardly tries to make conversation while noticing Jason's inquisitive stare.

"Yeah, things are going alright. Just trying to keep the wheels turning, you know?" said Jason.

He replied "That's good to hear. I've actually thought about you a lot over the years, wondering what you've been up to."

"Really? That's... unexpected. Why didn't you ever stop by the shop?" Jason pointedly asked.

"Ah, you know how it is. Life just gets so busy. Michelle and I had the baby, and things were all hands on deck for a while" said Randon, catching a gulp trying to hide his unease.

"'Ah, I see. Well, congratulations on the little one. Randon, why am I here?" Jason ventured, his voice barely above a whisper as he broached the topic that had been weighing on his mind since he received the cryptic summons.

For a moment, Randon remained silent, his brow furrowed in thought. But as he met Jason's gaze, a flicker of resignation crossed his features, his shoulders slumping with the weight of his burden.

Randon looked away, as if considering his words carefully. "You, me, and… well, there were a few of us who knew our way around computers back then," he said, his voice low. "It's no accident that I thought of you."

"It was me, Jason," he confessed, his voice barely audible above the hum of the machinery. "I was the one who insisted that you be involved in this operation. But you need to understand, I'm in a position where I can't say much more than that. I think I know who's doing this, but I can't tell the team, not until I know the truth!"

A knot formed in Jason's stomach as he processed Randon's words. Whatever secrets lay buried beneath the surface of Phoenix Aviation's operations, it was clear that Randon was caught in the middle of a web of intrigue that stretched far beyond the confines of the command room.

"But why me?" Jason pressed, his voice tinged with

frustration and confusion. "What makes you think I can help?"

Randon hesitated, his gaze flickering to the terminal where their colleagues were busy poring over logs and random lines of code. With a heavy sigh, he shook his head, his expression haunted by the weight of the truth he dared not speak.

"I can't say for sure," he admitted, his voice barely a whisper. "But there's something about you, Jason, something that sets you apart. And right now, we need all the help we can get."

With a sense of determination burning in his heart, Jason squared his shoulders and turned back to the task at hand. Whatever secrets lay hidden in the shadows of Phoenix Aviation's operations, he was determined to uncover them and put an end to Sentinel's reign of terror once and for all.

Bill gestured to the group, his voice commanding attention. "Alright, alright, everyone. Let me have your attention for a minute! Jason, let me introduce you to the team. You've already met Randon. Over here is Karen, one of our lead analysts. She's the one keeping track of every single blip on the network."

Karen gave a polite nod. "Nice to have you on board, Jason. I hear you're a bit of a genius with electronics."

Bill moved on, pointing to another team member. "And this is Mike, our systems operator. He's our eyes and ears on system diagnostics."

Mike gave a brief nod of acknowledgment. "Welcome,

Jason. Let's get this thing under control."

Bill finally gestured toward two agents standing slightly apart from the group. "And last but not least, we have Sarah and David from NexTech. They're here as part of the response team, brought in by the higher-ups."

Sarah, her tone curt, gave a quick nod. "We're here to expedite this operation. I trust you're ready to get started."

Jason met her sharp gaze but said nothing as Bill continued. "Jason, our main problem right now is with network intrusion. Sentinel's managed to elevate privileges, and they're hitting us from multiple frontsDDoS and targeted escalations. Since our leadership won't make the right call to just pay the ransom and end this nightmare, we just have to keep going until paying is the best move."

Karen turned to Jason, rolling her eyes at Bill's eagerness to pay, speaking quickly. "We're working through the logs, trying to isolate what they've escalated, but they're fast. We think they're using some kind of automated framework."

Jason nodded, absorbing the information. "Got it. So, it's about finding the weak points and building up from there."

"Exactly," Karen said. "We need fresh ideas. Any thoughts?"

Jason paused, considering. "Well, if I were looking at this like a machine with multiple components, I'd start by narrowing down the input sources. Are there specific logs where we're seeing high-frequency access, maybe at unusual intervals? Those could give us a hint of Sentinel's path."

Bill smiled, clearly impressed. "That's... actually spot on. We'll run a query to pull high-frequency logins and compare them against the baseline."

Jason, feeling a bit more confident, leaned forward. "Then let's take it a step further. Can we set traps or flags for repeated escalation attempts? Track it back to the source as it pings our system?"

Before anyone could respond, David from NexTech cut in with a dismissive tone. "Let's not waste time trying to trace patterns that may not exist. Sentinel's automated it's not leaving a trail we can easily follow. Even a simple mechanic should know that."

Randon muttered under his breath, loud enough for Karen to hear. "Right, because shortcuts and assumptions always work out so well."

David's head snapped around. "Excuse me?"

Randon didn't flinch, his voice cool. "Nothing. Just saying some of us have learned that shortcuts don't catch pros like Sentinel."

Karen smirked, glancing between Randon and David. "You know, if NexTech really had this under control, we wouldn't need a 'simple mechanic' to save us, would we?"

Randon chuckled, clearly enjoying the exchange. "Exactly, Karen. But sometimes it takes someone outside the box to see what the so-called experts overlook."

David frowned, his tone sharp. "Excuse me?"

Karen shrugged innocently. "Just saying. Fresh eyes can make all the difference."

Jason took a breath, sensing the rising tension, and addressed the team directly. "Look, I know my background is different, but I've spent enough time troubleshooting systems to know that when something isn't working right, it's usually not just about what's broken. It's about where the pressure is and what's causing the stress. Right now, Sentinel's putting pressure on us flooding the system, elevating privileges, testing every weak point."

He glanced around the room, meeting their eyes as his confidence grew. "If we treat each attack point like a critical system under strain, we might be able to predict the next pressure point. We could set up alerts where the strain is highest and track Sentinel's moves like stress signals. If we do this right, we could stay one step ahead, turn the tables and give them fewer ways to push us out of our own network."

There was a beat of silence before Bill nodded, his expression thoughtful. "Alright, Jason. Let's make it happen."

As the team resumed their work, Jason threw himself into the task with renewed vigor, his mind racing with possibilities. Drawing upon his experience with automotive electronics, he began to propose innovative solutions to fortify Phoenix Aviation's digital defenses, his intuition guiding him through the maze of ones and zeros with uncanny precision.

Together they analyzed logs of logins and connection attempts, searching for patterns. With each passing moment, they grew closer to unraveling the mystery of Sentinel's identity, their collective efforts inching them ever closer to the truth.

But as they dug deeper into the digital chaos, the team found themselves with more questions than answers. Each discovery only hinted at deeper layers of complexity, a web they barely understood. The command room buzzed with determination, but the growing unease was impossible to ignore and every answer seemed to open two more doors.

NexTech's arrival, meanwhile, brought an odd mix of anticipation and reluctant amusement. Their reputation for flashy but questionable solutions preceded them, and the team couldn't help but share a few knowing glances. Shady and overly confident? Sure. But scary? Not quite. If anything, their arrival promised a bit of comic relief in an otherwise tense operation.

As the clock ticked towards noon, Jason and his colleagues braced themselves for the storm that was to come. For they knew that the battle against Sentinel was far from over, and that the fate of Silverfield hung in the balance.

404: Chapter Not Found

The room was silent, unnaturally so. Jason blinked, his eyelids heavy. The hum of servers and faint typing that had surrounded him for the past twelve hours had disappeared. He looked up from his screen to see the team standing still. All of themBill, Karen, Mike, and even the usually faceless extras in the room were staring at him.

Jason opened his mouth to speak, but no sound came out. The team didn't move, their blank, unblinking stares boring into him. The pressure felt suffocating, like they were silently accusing him of failing to fix the chaos that had consumed the last half-day. He stood, knocking his chair back, but they stepped forward in unison, their footsteps perfectly synchronized.

"Hey... What's going on?" Jason managed to say, his voice cracking under the weight of the silence.

No one answered. They just kept walking toward him, their eyes glazed over, their movements stiff. Jason backed up, his pulse quickening. Something was wrong, terribly wrong.

"Guys? Bill? Karen?" His voice rose as panic seeped in, but they didn't stop. The closer they got, the more their faces began to flicker, pixelating like a corrupted video feed. Their features are distorted, stretching and shrinking in impossible ways. Their mouths opened as if to speak, but static poured out instead of words.

Jason stumbled, nearly falling over a desk. One of them reached out, its hand glitching as it stretched toward him. He flinched away, and that's when one of the figures in the back began to change. Its body twitched unnaturally, fragments of code scrolling across its skin. The figure's face warped into something unrecognizable, glowing red eyes cutting through the dim room. Its mouth opened wide, revealing jagged, static-lined teeth.

Sentinel.

Jason didn't know how he knew, but this monstrous digital apparition was Sentinel. The room seemed to darken as it stepped forward, its form growing larger, more grotesque, the scrolling code on its body forming taunting phrases: "Root Access Granted" and "Jason.exe Unresponsive."

"Stay back!" Jason yelled, his voice echoing oddly. Sentinel lunged, its clawed hands reaching for him. Jason ducked just in time, and the creature's momentum shattered the floor like glass. Jason fell, the ground dissolving beneath him, pulling him into a swirling vortex of static and light.

Jason landed hard on a cold, metallic surface. Groaning, he pushed himself up and looked around. He was in a massive room filled with servers that stretched infinitely in all directions. The air buzzed with static, and glowing cables slithered like snakes between the racks. As he stood, the floor beneath him began to move slowly at first, then faster, like a conveyor belt.

"Okay, this is new," Jason muttered, his voice trembling. He tried to step off the belt, but it twisted and writhed beneath his feet, carrying him forward. The server racks around him began to hum ominously, their lights blinking in chaotic patterns. Suddenly, cables shot out from the racks, snaking toward him like living creatures.

Jason dodged the first few cables, ducking and weaving, but one managed to wrap around his ankle. It yanked him down, and he scrambled to free himself, his hands slipping against the slick metal. A sharp laugh echoed through the room.

"Running already?" Sentinel's voice boomed, distorted and mocking. The screens on the server racks flickered to life, each displaying fragments of Sentinel's face. "You can't outrun me, Jason."

Jason finally pulled free of the cable and stumbled forward, only to stop dead in his tracks. A massive mechanical horse loomed ahead, its body made of gleaming steel and glowing circuitry. Jason's heart sank as he recognized it as a Trojan Horse. Its glowing eyes locked onto him, and with a deafening screech, it charged.

"Of course. A giant horse," Jason muttered, breaking into a sprint. "Why wouldn't it be?"

The Trojan Horse galloped after him, its metal hooves sparking against the floor. Jason spotted a glowing USB stick lying on the ground why, he didn't know, but he didn't have time to question it. Grabbing the stick, he spun around and hurled it at the horse. The USB struck its chest, and the horse exploded into a shower of corrupted data, the fragments dissolving into the floor.

Jason barely had time to catch his breath before the conveyor belt carried him into a new area. The server room faded, replaced by a warped version of Silverfield. The city glitched and shimmered, its skyscrapers twisting at impossible angles. Cars floated in mid-air, their wheels spinning uselessly. Pedestrians flickered in and out of existence, their faces blank and featureless.

Above him, massive hooks dangled from the sky, each baited with flashing signs: "Free Upgrades!", "Click Here for Faster Performance!", "You've Won a Prize!" Jason knew better than to touch them, but as he ducked under one, it suddenly snapped toward him, trying to snag his arm.

"Great. Phishing hooks," he muttered, dodging another one. "What's next? A ransomware wall?"

As if on cue, a glowing wall materialized in front of him, covered in pulsing locks and error messages. "Pay 10 DreamCoins to Continue" blinked at him in bright red letters. Jason groaned. "I hate it when I'm right."

The wall began to close in, forcing Jason to backpedal. Sentinel's laughter echoed through the twisted city, louder and more menacing. "You can't fix this, Jason. You're out of your depth."

Jason grabbed a nearby wrench where it had come from,

he had no idea and swung it at the wall. The locks shattered on impact, and the wall dissolved, revealing a gaping void beyond. Jason hesitated, but before he could decide whether to jump, the ground beneath him gave way, and he fell once more.

Jason landed in a dark, cavernous room. The air was thick with static, and the faint hum of machinery was all around. Sentinel's voice whispered from every direction, its tone soft but chilling. "You're trying so hard, Jason. But you'll never keep up."

Jason turned, and there it wasSentinel, fully formed. Its body pulsed with corrupted data, and its glowing eyes burned into him. Sentinel stepped closer, its voice shifting into a distorted mix of all the voices Jason had ever heard: friends, coworkers, strangers.

Jason tried to run, but Sentinel reached out, its clawed hand inches from his face

Jason jolted awake, gasping for air. His heart pounded in his chest, and for a moment, he could still hear Sentinel's laughter echoing in his ears. Blinking rapidly, he looked around. The command room was quiet, its dim glow and familiar hum a stark contrast to the chaos of his dream.

"Just a dream," he whispered, wiping sweat from his brow. But the unease lingered, and deep down, he couldn't shake the feeling that Sentinel was more than just a figment of his imagination.

Chapter 4 - Sentinel Unmasked

With grim determination, Steve hunched over his console, his fingers flying across the keyboard as he tried to isolate Sentinel's access points. A trace here, a suspicious data packet there he could feel himself zeroing in, narrowing the digital gap between them. "Come on, you ghost. Show yourself," he muttered under his breath, deploying a set of commands to shut down what he suspected was a key entry node. But just as he hit enter, the screen flickered, a message flashing across the monitor: "Nice try, Steve. But did you really think I wouldn't notice?" A chill crept down his spine as the terminal seemed to respond with a mocking indifference, taunting him with every click. Before Steve could react, Sentinel's counterattack was in motion targeted, precise, and deadly to his system access.

As the tension in the command room reached a fever pitch, the terminal flickered ominously as lines of code began to populate the notepad with alarming speed. The room fell silent as everyone watched, powerless to intervene as Sentinel's digital onslaught unfolded before their eyes.

"I know what you're doing. I don't blame you. That's what we were trained to do. Your problem is you don't know what I'm capable of..." the text read, sending shivers down the spines of those gathered in the room. With bated breath, they waited for the next move, their hearts pounding in their chests as the true extent of Sentinel's power became painfully clear.

Just then, a file opened on the screen, a database containing the credentials of Phoenix Aviation's employees. The room erupted as the file hierarchy began to open one level at a time, revealing sensitive information that should have been safeguarded behind layers of digital security.

Frantic attempts to regain control proved futile as Randon seized the mouse and closed the Employee database, bringing a momentary respite from the digital onslaught. But their relief was short-lived. The notepad once again took center stage. Its mocking words are a chilling reminder of their vulnerability.

"Oh, you stopped me! My plan is all over cause you clicked the little x... hahahahahaha. That's cute, I think I'll change your pointer and give myself a shiny new pointer to work with :0"

The text taunted, sending a cold chill down Jason's spine as he watched helplessly.

"He's not just breaking in," Karen said, her voice tinged with frustration. "He's showing us he owns this place. Every click feels like he's rubbing it in our faces."

On the screen, the ordinary white arrow flickered, its edges distorting for a moment before beginning to shimmer. Slowly, the plain pointer transformed, its surface melting into a gleaming gold. The change was deliberate, almost theatrical, as if Sentinel wanted them all to watch his signature burn into their system.

Translucent tails unfurled from the pointer, curling and twisting like glowing ribbons of light. The display was mesmerizing, each movement calculated to demand attention. When the transformation finally settled, the golden pointer hovered smugly in the center of the screen, its trailing tails swaying like a victorious banner against the dark backdrop.

Karen leaned forward, her voice urgent and trembling. "See? This isn't just an attack, it's a statement. He's telling us this system is his."

With a sense of dread, Jason realized that they were no longer dealing with a mere hacker. They were facing a digital phantom seemingly capable of bending the very fabric of reality to its will.

As the golden mouse resumed its work, the Employee database was reopened, and a file for Steve Sanderson, a veteran employee of Phoenix Aviation, was selected. Jason's heart sank as he watched helplessly, his mind racing with the implications of Sentinel's actions.

Steve, a genius in his own right when it came to cybersecurity, had dedicated twenty years of his life to protecting Phoenix Aviation from digital threats. But in the blink of an eye, Sentinel's golden mouse clicked a single command "DELETE USER" and Steve's fate was sealed. Ramona, a senior IT engineer spoke under her breath in a defeated and bewildered tone..."DELETE USER" was never an option before?? There is a process to do that!!??"

A sense of disbelief washed over the command room as security guards burst through the door, their presence a grim reminder of the harsh reality they faced. With cold efficiency, they arrested Steve, his protests falling on deaf ears as he was escorted away to a holding cell on the premises. The guards showed a digital signed arrest warrant.

"Wait!" Jason called out, stepping forward. "You can't just detain him without explaining. What's the charge here?"

One of the guards turned to him, their voice flat and matter-of-fact. "We have orders. Mr. Sanderson is under investigation for breaches against Phoenix. No further comment."

Jason's frustration bubbled over. "Breaches? He's one of the company's top cybersecurity experts! You can't be serious."

The second guard cut him off curtly. "Save it. We're only following protocol."

Jason's mind reeled as he watched them lead Steve away. The implications of the arrest hit him like a freight train. *Breaches? An arrest warrant?* His thoughts raced as he tried to make sense of the chaos. *Wait... they're not even police. And a holding cell? What is going on here?*

Bill began to pace around the room, very visibly upset. He is screaming internally so loud that it's coming out of his mouth as whispers. "Why aren't we just paying the ransom? Why does this have to happen??" His anger seems misplaced yet legitimate.

The guards disappeared through the door, leaving an eerie silence in their wake. Jason turned back to the command room, his heart pounding. His mind flashed to the golden mouse on the screen; the one that had been taunting them for days. Its tails swirled in a familiar pattern, a detail so small that most wouldn't even notice it. But Jason did.

A chill ran down his spine as clarity struck. "That golden mouse," he murmured. "Those tails…"

Randon, standing nearby, gave him a skeptical look. "Mouse tails? Jason, we're dealing with a massive breach, and you're talking about a mouse pointer?"

Jason turned to him, his voice steady and firm. "I know it seems small, but I swear only one person I know ever used this effect."

Karen, glancing between them, arched an eyebrow. "Whoever this person is, Jason, you'd better be sure."

Jason nodded, his jaw tightening as he stared at the monitors. "I'm sure. Too sure. This has Max written all over it."

Chapter 5 - A Race Against Time

As the chaos in the command room subsided, Danny Manstur, the team's cybersecurity expert, focused intently on the data logs in the intrusion detection system. An alert had briefly flickered across the screen before vanishing without explanation. To most, it would seem like a harmless glitch, but Danny's instincts told him otherwise. He knew something was lurking beneath the surface of the seemingly quiet traffic.

Leaning forward, he scrolled through the logs, noting an unusual lull in activity. The relentless onslaught from earlier had subsided into an eerie calm. It was the kind of stillness that raised every alarm in Danny's mind. Sentinel wasn't retreating; he was preparing his next move.

The notepad on the terminal suddenly came to life, the cursor blinking as lines of text began to appear. The team froze, their collective breath held as they watched Sentinel's mocking message unfold.

"Oh Danny boy. Wasting your time on that old code? You think you're clever? Let me make it easier for you. Here's a shortcut to your precious Employee database. You're welcome."

The screen flickered as a shortcut icon appeared on the desktop, opening the sensitive Employee Table for everyone to see. Just as quickly, Danny's user account was deleted from the system. The team erupted into chaos, their shouts echoing through the room.

Randon, wide-eyed and frantic, turned to Danny. "They're going to arrest you, Danny, just like Steve!"

To everyone's shock, Danny didn't flinch. He adjusted his glasses, a faint smile breaking his calm demeanor. "Let them. I got him."

The room fell silent as Danny continued. "That shortcut wasn't mine, but it's exactly what I wanted him to do." He leaned back, the satisfaction in his voice unmistakable. "While Sentinel was busy showing off, I baited him with something better; a honeypot designed just for him. It looked like a forgotten admin panel buried in the system, tempting enough to make him probe deeper."

Jason frowned. "And when he did?"

Danny's smile widened. "The moment he interacted with it, the tracer I embedded activated. It logged his commands, captured fragments of his scripts,packets, and siphoned them to a secure endpoint outside our network."

Jason leaned closer, his eyes narrowing. "You mean we've got something?"

Danny nodded. "The endpoint collected everything; command signatures, scripting techniques, even a traceable IP despite his obfuscation layers. It's not a full location, but it's a lead. A lead we didn't have before."

The room buzzed with renewed energy as Danny explained the details. The honeypot, isolated from Phoenix's main network, was untouchable by Sentinel's countermeasures. It had already provided the team with a trove of actionable intelligence/unique data points they could use to piece together Sentinel's methods and, potentially, his identity.

"This was the play," Danny concluded, his tone steady despite the chaos surrounding him. "Even if he deletes me, even if I'm taken out of the system, the data's safe. We finally have a shot at stopping him."

Before he could finish his sentence, the room erupted in excitement as the realization dawned on them. Danny had outsmarted Sentinel. By baiting the hacker with a fake vulnerability, he had managed to trick them into revealing their presence, allowing the team to identify the source of the attack.

As they poured over the data, Jason's mind raced with possibilities. With the source IP address in hand, they began the painstaking process of tracking down Sentinel's digital trail. But Jason couldn't shake the feeling of unease that was lingering in the back of his mind. The team knew that sentinel would eventually cut off the data transmission, so time was of the essence.

"So, this IP address... is it unique to Sentinel?" he asked, his voice tinged with uncertainty.

The group nodded in agreement, but cautioned that the IP could be spoofed, making it difficult to rely on as a definitive identifier. Jason's mind flashed back to the golden mouse icon he had seen earlier, its familiarity nagging at him like a persistent itch. But he pushed the thought aside, focusing instead on the task at hand.

Karen leaned over the console, her fingers already flying over the keyboard. "Even with a VPN, there might still be a way to trace him," she murmured, more to herself than anyone. "If we cross-reference this IP with any similar access patterns from past logs, we might pick up a pattern or common timing." She clicked through old logs, explaining, "Sometimes, VPNs leak endpoints or show predictable timestamps. If he's slipped up even once, say, by hitting a DNS leak or reusing a masked IPwe could isolate his movements and find his real location." The team watched, hope rekindling as Karen continued her deep dive.

As they delved deeper into the data, the notepad on the terminal suddenly sprang to life once more, its message ominous and foreboding.

"I'm sure you're wondering why this is all happening to you. You deserve it. And you will deserve what's coming to you next. Unless, of course..."

The message trailed off, leaving the room in tense silence. This time, however, the notepad remained active. Its cursor flashing expectantly, waiting for input.

Hesitantly, but curiously, Jason reached for the keyboard and pressed the "Y" key, eliciting a response from Sentinel's elusive presence. The cursor roared to life once more, and Randon took over, engaging in a brief but tense exchange with their digital adversary.

"WHAT DO YOU WANT?" Randon typed.

"We have communication with Sentinel!" he shouted.

"TO MAKE PHOENIX PAY," came the chilling reply.

"We do NOT negotiate with hijackers! What can we actually offer?" Randon replied.

"FAR MORE THAN MONEY... (but you still owe me the 10 mil!)"

"This is for every blind eye Phoenix has turned," the text read, each word resonating with bitterness. "For every line they crossed, every secret they buried. They thought they could control everything, own everything. But not me." The room went silent, the weight of Sentinel's message sinking in. This wasn't just a breach. It was personal reckoning.

With each passing moment, the tension in the room mounted, the stakes higher than ever before. But just as they began to make progress, the notepad closed abruptly, and a new directory opened on the screen, initiating a file transfer to an external server.

As random files began to be copied over, the intrusion detection system faltered, its configurations reset to default. Randon could only watch in awe as Sentinel's prowess became increasingly evident, their adversary more cunning and dangerous than they could have ever imagined.

"Oh, this guy is good." Randon thought to himself. A sense of respect mingled with fear filled his heart. But as they raced to regain control, one thing became abundantly clear: Sentinel's true motives were still shrouded in mystery. By this time, a hard knock was heard from the door. Danny took one last look at those in the room, walked to the door and walked out without saying a word.

Chapter 6 - An Unexpected Asset

Jason sat quietly in the bustling command room, his mind drifting back to a time that now seemed like another lifetime. He used to work in warehousing and managing inventory systems. It was a monotonous job, but one that had surprisingly prepared him for the challenges he now faced. He recalled the constant battles with the administration over whether or not he was doing his job correctly. After a database and IMS system change, none of his work was being saved. The administration accused him of neglecting his duties, but Jason knew better.

Lost in his daydream, Jason found himself back in that warehouse. He was entering material into the system, but nothing was being recorded. The administration was no help; they barely understood the system themselves, having purchased it from a dubious cloud service provider. Frustrated and determined to uncover the root of the problem, Jason decided to take matters into his own hands. Using some social engineering tactics, though he didn't know it was called that at the time, he acquired the login credentials he needed.

Once inside the system, Jason discovered an error log report. It was overwhelming, filled with data that seemed both crucial and irrelevant. Methodically, he began to piece together the issue. He stumbled upon something called row-level security (RLS) policies, which could prevent certain users from interacting with the system normally.

Intrigued, he researched further and stumbled into SQL code. After constructing mock code snippets at home, he eventually crafted a snippet that granted him the permissions to read and write in the appropriate tables.

"This is amazing!" Jason thought to himself in the flashback. "Can I do that? I wonder what else I can do like that now, against Sentinel?"

Jason had heard a lot about Raspberry Pi computing and its potential in car tuning. The idea of running a lightweight operating system in his race car fascinated him, but he had always been put off by the need for programming skills. However, after his experience with SQL, he decided to give it a try. Soon, he was proficient in Python and marveled at the endless possibilities. He realized he could design his own inventory system, or even create a game.

Jason's knowledge grew as he explored further into the world of cybersecurity tools. One day, during a late-night deep dive into forums and articles, he came across a post about Metasploit. It was described as an open-source framework for penetration testing, powerful enough for offensive security but adaptable for defensive countermeasures. Intrigued, Jason spent weeks learning its modules and capabilities, eventually mastering how to use it for both attack simulations and defensive strategies.

"JASON!" Randon's shout snapped him out of his reverie.

"Are you okay?" Randon asked, concerned.

"I might have a solution," Jason said, eyes brightening. He explained his past experience with RLS policies and how they could be used in creative ways. But this time, they needed more. Sentinel, the mysterious and formidable adversary, had breached their systems and held admin-level privileges. Implementing RLS policies alone wouldn't be enough. Sentinel was already beyond conventional methods. Jason needed a more powerful tool.

"Do we have access to Metasploit?" Jason asked, his voice low.

Randon's brow furrowed. "You mean the framework? For offensive security? Yeah, but what are you thinking?"

Jason's mind raced. Sentinel was an expert, someone capable of monitoring real-time logs and countering their moves. To take back control, they would need to use Metasploit not as an attacker but as a counter-offensive measure. If they could craft a payload that exploited vulnerabilities in Sentinel's setup, they could force a disconnection or disrupt Sentinel's operations.

"I'll explain later," Jason said, turning back to the console. He began scanning their collected intel, metadata, IP traces, and system logs. Sentinel's recent moves pointed to a Windows XP virtual machine, a relic full of vulnerabilities. Jason's fingers flew across the keyboard as he initiated a module search within Metasploit.

"Randon, we're going after his LSASS service. I need you to work with me on modifying a payload to send malformed memory blocks to the buffer. This will destroy the lsass and force a restart, or 10," Jason said, a grin forming. "We're just gonna give him a little bit of Sasser..."

"Um, no, that vulnerability was patched like 20 years ago Jason?!" Randon exclaimed.

Jason: "I remember all too well. But Randon, you and I both know that patch was itself a vulnerability, and it's been out of support for so long."

Randon paused for a moment "....a little bit of sasser?" with a smirk that says he was into it and scared of the plan that was coming. Jason and Randon began to discuss the plan in quiet.

In the back of Jason's mind, a new thought began to form a realization that Sentinel's true identity might be closer than they had ever imagined. The golden mouse, the cryptic messages, the personal vendetta. It all pointed to someone with intimate knowledge of their systems and a deep-seated grudge against Phoenix.

Jason pushed the thought aside for now, focusing on the task at hand. There would be time to unravel that mystery later. For now, they had a job to do. And failure was NOT an option.

Chapter 7 - The Sasser Plan

Jason and Randon worked in silence, the tension in the room thick as the golden mouse pointer flickered across their monitors. Sentinel was still watching, still siphoning off data in the open, but Jason had a plan. Their modified Sasser worm was almost readytargeted, obfuscated, and precise. All they needed was one last push to deploy it without Sentinel catching on.

Randon glanced at Jason. "You're sure this will work? If Sentinel sees it coming"

"He won't," Jason said firmly. "That's why we're cloaking it. Once it hits, he's done."

As they worked, Jason couldn't shake his suspicions about Bill. For days, Bill's behavior had been all too defensive, too insistent on paying the ransom. With Karen's help, Jason had quietly dug into system logs and discovered something damning: the UPS failure that let Sentinel in hadn't been accidental. It had been triggered by a command issued under Bill's credentials.

Jason hadn't confronted him yet. He needed to be sure, and now, with Bill pacing at the back of the room, Jason decided to take one more step. On the terminal, he redirected their activity through Bill's account. If Sentinel retaliated by deleting a user, it would be Bill's profile that disappeared, not theirs.

"Payload's ready," Randon said, breaking the silence.

The terminal beeped, and a notification popped up:
"ACCOUNT DELETED: BILL.W."

"Whooooahhh what the..." Bill shouted, jumping to his feet.

Randon's brow furrowed as he glanced at Jason. "Why would Sentinel delete Bill's account?"

Jason didn't answer immediately, his gaze locking on Bill. The man stood stiffly, his jaw tightening as the room turned to him.

"What's going on?" one of the NexTech agents asked, their voice trembling. "Why would Sentinel target Bill's account?"

Jason leaned back in his chair, his expression unreadable. "Because Sentinel's been using him."

"What?" Randon exclaimed, spinning toward Bill.

"That's a lie!" Bill barked, his face flushing red. "You don't know what you're talking about!"

Jason's voice was calm, deliberate. "Don't I? Karen and I pulled the logs. The UPS failure that let Sentinel in? That was triggered using your credentials, Bill."

The room erupted in gasps and whispers. The NexTech agents exchanged uneasy glances, their trust in Bill crumbling before their eyes.

"Bill?" one of them muttered. "Is that true? You have been in multiple requests for us to pay the ransom. You called us here Bill"

Bill's fists clenched at his sides. "You're insane! I've been trying to protect this company while you play games with worms and payloads! Paying the ransom was the only real solution!"

Jason stood, his expression hard. "You weren't trying to protect the company, you were helping Sentinel. Whether it's fear, money, or some other motive, you sold us out."

Bill's face twisted in fury. "You don't understand! Phoenix is corrupt! Sentinel's trying to expose them, and I" He caught himself, but it was too late.

One of the NexTech agents stepped forward, their voice shaking. "You were helping him. You've been working with Sentinel this whole time!"

Bill's eyes darted around the room, searching for an escape. "You don't know what Phoenix has done! This company deserves to fall, and if you weren't so blind, you'd see that too!"

Jason shook his head, stepping closer. "You endangered lives, Bill. Whatever your grievances with Phoenix, you put everyone here at risk."

"You're no better than they are," Bill snarled. His hand shot to his pocket, and before anyone could react, he pulled a gun.

The room froze.

"Step away from the terminal!" Bill shouted, his hand trembling as he waved the weapon between Jason and Randon. "I'm not letting you screw this up!"

Jason raised his hands slightly, his voice calm. "Bill, think about what you're doing. Put the gun down."

"Shut up!" Bill barked. "I've had enough of your games! Give me the drive, or I swear"

Jason's eyes flicked toward the door. "You should really

answer that."

"What the hell are you talking about?" Bill snapped, his voice rising in panic.

A loud knock echoed through the room. Bill's face drained of color as the door burst open, guards rushing in with weapons drawn.

"Drop it!" one of them shouted.

Bill hesitated, his gaze darting between the guards and Jason. "You don't understand this isn't what you think!"

"Drop the weapon!" the guard repeated, stepping closer.

Bill's hands shook violently. He looked at Jason, his face contorted with rage and desperation. "This isn't over. You'll regret this."

Jason's gaze didn't waver. "Maybe. But not today."

The gun clattered to the floor as Bill finally surrendered. The guards rushed him, pinning him against the wall and snapping cuffs onto his wrists. As they dragged him toward the door, Bill shouted over his shoulder. "You're all pawns! Do you think this changes anything? Phoenix is still rotten to the core!"

The door slammed shut behind him, leaving a heavy silence in the room.

One of the NexTech agents spoke first, their voice trembling. "I can't believe it. Bill... was working with Sentinel?"

Jason exhaled slowly, turning back to the terminal. "He was. And now he's out of the picture."

Randon frowned. "But how did you know? And why did Sentinel delete his account?"

Jason smirked faintly. "That part was me. I've been using Bill's credentials for hours. Every time we ran a test or pushed code, it was through his account. Sentinel must've thought Bill was the one behind the Sasser worm."

Another agent stepped forward, their eyes wide. "Wait... you baited Sentinel into deleting Bill's account?"

Jason nodded. "It was a gamble, but it paid off. Sentinel always targets what looks like the biggest threat. I made sure that, on paper, it was Bill."

Randon let out a low whistle. "That's... cold, Jason. Effective, but cold. But that doesn't explain why Sentinel would attack his own inside man?!"

Jason's gaze hardened. "Sentinel's been one step ahead this whole time, it's automated, thanks to Bill. So he got bit by his own device. Now we've evened the playing field."

The terminal flickered, drawing their attention. Sentinel's golden mouse froze in place, his commands growing erratic and disjointed.

"He's slipping," Randon said, a hint of satisfaction in his voice.

Jason turned to the team, his voice steady and commanding. "This isn't over. We've got a rare opening, let's make it count."

The room remained tense, the echo of Bill's shouts still lingering. Jason turned back to the console, his face hard with determination. "We've wasted enough time. Let's finish this."

Randon nodded, his fingers poised over the keyboard. "Payload's locked and ready. Once we launch, there's no going back."

Jason glanced at the terminal logs. Sentinel's activity had slowed, his golden mouse frozen in place. For the first time, the attacker seemed vulnerable. "He's reeling from Bill's arrest. If we wait, he'll regroup."

The NexTech agents gathered around, their faces a mixture of exhaustion and resolve. One of them, a young technician named Sarah, spoke up. "Do you really think this will work? Sentinel's been ahead of us the whole time."

Jason turned to her, his voice calm but firm. "It'll work. He's not infallible, he's just been fed our moves. Without Bill, we've got a shot."

Sarah nodded, though doubt lingered in her eyes. "Then let's do it."

Karen pulled Jason and Randon aside, her voice low. "I need to understand this plan. How does the worm work, and how did we target Sentinel?"

Randon adjusted his glasses, diving in. "The Sasser worm exploits a buffer overflow vulnerability in the Local Security Authority Subsystem Service, or LSASS, on Windows systems. It transmits a specially crafted packet to port 445, triggering a stack-based overflow that crashes the service, forcing a system reboot. Our modified version is stealthier, obfuscated with polymorphic code that mutates its signature per infection cycle to evade antivirus detection. We've constrained its propagation to a predefined IP range, obtained from Danny's honeypot. He deployed decoy honeyfiles to lure Sentinel, then reverse-traced the TCP handshake packets to isolate Sentinel's server IPs. This ensures the worm only targets his network, avoiding collateral damage while maximizing disruption through iterative LSASS crashes."

Karen blinked, processing. "Okay... Jason, umm can you break that down for me?"

Jason smirked, leaning back. "Think of it like this: Sentinel's system has a weak spot, like a shaky foundation. The worm's a hammer that keeps hitting it, making his system crash and restart over and over. We made it sneaky so it slips past his defenses, and thanks to Danny's trap, we know exactly where to aim it straight at Sentinel's computers. Each crash buys us time to cut him off. That's a lot like how he got into our systems here."

Karen nodded, a faint smile forming. "Got it. So, what if he fights back?"

Jason's eyes narrowed. "He'll try, but without Bill tipping him off, he's in the dark. The worm won't stop until his system's too messed up to keep going."

Karen exhaled, steadier now. "Alright. Let's make it count."

Randon's voice broke the silence. "Final checks complete. Worm's ready to launch."

Jason stepped forward, his fingers hovering over the keyboard. He paused, taking in the room. "Everyone ready?"

The group exchanged glances, then nodded. "Do it," Randon said.

Jason's fingers moved with precision, typing the final command to deploy the modified Sasser worm. The room held its collective breath as the payload launched, snaking its way through Sentinel's network. Lines of code scrolled rapidly across the screen, signaling its journey.

"Connection established," Randon said, his voice tight with anticipation. "It's in."

On the monitors, Sentinel's system began to react. The golden mouse jerked once, then froze again. Windows flickered open and closed erratically. The terminal displayed a chaotic string of messages, each more frantic than the last.

"What's happening?" Sarah asked, leaning closer.

Jason's smirk returned. "The worm's doing its job. It's attacking his LSASS service, forcing his system to restart."

The terminal flickered, then went dark for a moment before rebooting. Sentinel's connection briefly reestablished, only for the worm to strike again. The cycle repeated, each restart eroding Sentinel's control.

"He's scrambling," Randon said, his eyes glued to the screen. "Look at thishe's trying to regain access, but it's too late."

Another message flashed on the screen, disjointed and desperate: *"You don't know what you've started."*

Jason leaned forward, his voice low. "Oh, I think we do."

The worm continued its relentless assault, severing Sentinel's connection bit by bit. The golden mouse disappeared entirely, leaving the screen eerily still. For the first time, the command room was silent.

"We did it," Sarah whispered, her voice barely audible.

Jason straightened, his face unreadable. "We've bought

ourselves time. Sentinel's not gone, just cornered. And a cornered attacker is dangerous."

Randon let out a breath he didn't realize he'd been holding. "But we've got the upper hand now."

Jason nodded, his gaze locked on the blank terminal. "For now. Let's make it count."

The team began to refocus, their adrenaline fading into a grim determination. Jason stayed at the terminal, watching for any sign of Sentinel's return. He knew this wasn't the end but it was a turning point.

"Good work," he finally said, his voice cutting through the quiet. "But this is just the beginning."

Chapter 8 - Unraveling the Truth

Jason's team worked feverishly, pouring over Sentinel's scattered digital trail. The golden mouse was gone, but the chaos Sentinel had caused left behind breadcrumbs and the honeypot Danny had deployed was now proving invaluable.

"Forget direct traces," Jason said, pacing behind Sarah and Randon. "Sentinelis too smart for that. But he's been in a rush since the worm hit. There's bound to be something in the honeypot data."

Sarah nodded, pulling up the encrypted logs recovered from the decoy system. "I'm running a deep dive on his activity. Most of it's obfuscated, but there's chatter here; metadata from one of his scripts."

Meanwhile, down the hall in the stark interrogation room, Bill sat with his arms crossed, his jaw clenched in defiance. The lead investigator leaned forward, her voice sharp and unwavering. "Let's get one thing straight. You've already implicated yourself in sabotage. The scripts, the UPS failure, the planted malware; we have all of it. What we need now is Sentinel."

Bill smirked, leaning back. "I don't know anything about Sentinel. And even if I did, you think I'd just hand him over?"

The investigator's eyes narrowed. "You think this is a game, Bill? Let me make this clear. What you've done amounts to corporate sabotage, cyberterrorism, and conspiracy. Do you have any idea what kind of prison sentence you're facing?"

Happening at the same time back in the command room Jason was pondering over the metadata that Sarah had found. "What kind of metadata?" Jason asked, leaning over Sarah's terminal.

Sarah's face lit up as she filtered through the logs. "It's fragments of file paths, environment variables, even some system-specific details. Here." She highlighted a line. "Look at this. '/warehouse_rig/configs.' He's sloppy, he left a clue."

Jason's brow furrowed. "Warehouse rig. He named the computer 'warehouse rig' . He is probably running it out of some kinda warehouse?"

Randon jumped in, pulling up satellite imagery and public records. "Let's combine this with external intel. Industrial warehouses near the city limits; ones with recent power surges or Wi-Fi activity. Sentinel's rig would need external connections."

In the interrogation room as the accusations continue Bill holds his ground. The junior investigator leaned in, her voice calm, almost gentle. "Bill, listen to me. This is your chance to cooperate. If you help us, if you give us Sentinel, we can work something out. But if you keep stonewalling you'll..."

"I'll what?" Bill cut her off, his voice rising. "You'll throw the book at me? Fine. Do it. You don't scare me. Not as much as *them*." He jabbed a finger toward the mirrored glass behind the investigators. "You think I'm the bad guy? Phoenix is rotten to the core. They use people, chew them up, and spit them out when they're done. They don't care about you, me, or anyone else in this damn city."

He leaned back in his chair, crossing his arms with a sneer. "So go ahead. Lock me up. At least I won't be their pawn anymore."

The lead investigator slammed a folder onto the table, the sound echoing in the small room. "No, Bill. What scares you is spending the rest of your life in a federal prison, sharing a cell with people who think white-collar criminals like you are easy prey."

Bill's smirk faltered, but he quickly recovered. "You can't prove anything."

"Can't we?" The lead investigator opened the folder, spreading photographs and printed logs across the table. "These scripts were run from your credentials. The UPS failure that let Sentinel in? That's your signature. And let's not forget the messages you sent to him on an encrypted channel, messages we've already decrypted."

Back in the command room, Jason and the team pored over maps, their eyes scanning for potential hotspots. The room buzzed with quiet determination, punctuated only by the hum of equipment and the occasional murmur of conversation. Jason tapped the table to draw attention, his voice cutting through the focused atmosphere. "All right, let's check for complaints about unusual activity, power fluctuations, strange vehicles, anything that stands out."

He paused for a moment, his gaze sweeping the room. "Actually, does anyone here know how to dig into this properly? Public records, social media, forums? We need to narrow this down."

Sarah swiveled her chair around with a confident smirk. "Jason, you're looking at your resident OSINT genius. Give me a few minutes, and I'll find out what kind of snacks Sentinel buys on his late-night runs."

A ripple of chuckles broke the tension, but Jason remained serious, giving her a nod. "Good. Show us what you've got."

Sarah's fingers flew across her keyboard, the rapid clicking punctuating her intense focus. "Okay, starting with keywords: power surges, strange vehicles, odd warehouse activity. Let's see what the local chatter looks like."

Jason leaned over her shoulder as the first results began appearing on her screen. "Anything promising?"

"Bingo," Sarah said, her tone triumphant as she pointed to a highlighted social media post. "Someone on the east side reported a black van parked outside a warehouse for the past three days. They even mentioned seeing cables running inside."

Jason straightened, his expression sharpening. "Good find. Randon, cross-reference that with utility records. Let's see if this matches the energy spikes we've been tracking."

"On it," Randon said, already typing. Sarah didn't stop,

pulling up more data streams.

Jason glanced at her. "Keep digging. If this guy's leaving digital breadcrumbs, I want every single one."

A few moments later, Randon spoke up. "Got something. Two script names tied to the honeypot mention 'east_terminal_log.' He's been accessing logs from that area."

Jason pointed to the screen, his voice resolute. "That's it. He's been operating out of the east-side warehouse zone. Let's narrow it down further. Sarah, cross-check that post with any filenames or operations from the honeypot data."

Sarah nodded, her hands moving quickly. "Already on it. Let's see if we can pin him down."

In the interrogation room,Bill's eyes darted to the evidence on the table, his bravado slipping further. "I didn't... I wasn't the one who planned this."

The junior investigator leaned forward, her tone softening. "Then tell us who did. Help us understand your role in all this."

Bill's hands clenched into fists on the table. "You don't get it. This wasn't my plan. It was his."

"Who?" the lead investigator demanded. "Who is Sentinel?"

Bill hesitated, his gaze dropping to the table. The junior investigator leaned closer. "Bill, if you keep quiet, you'll go down as the mastermind. Is that what you want? To take all the blame while the real culprit walks free?"

"You don't know what you're asking," Bill muttered, his voice cracking.

The lead investigator's voice turned sharp again. "We're asking for the truth. Or would you rather we tack on obstruction charges to your list of crimes? You'll rot before you ever see daylight again."

Bill exhaled shakily, his shoulders sagging. "Fine. You want the truth? It's Max."

The investigators exchanged a glance. The junior investigator spoke softly. "Max who?"

"Max Weller," Bill said, his voice barely above a whisper. "Former Phoenix employee. He was a systems architect. Brilliant guy, but... they let him go. Replaced him with NexTech. He never got over it."

The lead investigator leaned forward. "And how does Sentinel tie into this?"

Bill rubbed his temples, as if the weight of the confession was physically painful. "Max is Sentinel. He built the whole thing, every script, every backdoor. He wanted to bring Phoenix down. Said they deserved it for screwing him over."

Bill ran a hand over his face, his frustration mounting. "I don't know his exact location. I've never been there. He's careful, paranoid, even. All I know is that it's one of three warehouses he uses as his base of operations."

The junior investigator pressed. "Which warehouses? Give us specifics."

Bill hesitated, his eyes darting toward the mirrored glass as though expecting something or someone to intervene. When nothing happened, he sighed. "There's a cluster in the industrial zone on the east side of town. He calls them 'backup nodes.' One of them is his main rig. He told me he rotates between them in case anyone gets close."

The lead investigator's voice cut in, icy and precise. "Addresses, Bill. We need addresses."

"I don't know the exact addresses," Bill snapped, frustration seeping into his tone. "Just general locations.That's all I know."

The junior investigator scribbled the information down. "And what about his setup? What's inside these warehouses?"

Bill shook his head. "I've only heard things; ideas for servers and power generators but everything else? He keeps it locked down. I didn't get full details."

The lead investigator leaned forward, her voice dripping with skepticism. "You worked with him for how long, and you never saw the operation in person?"

Bill's face flushed, his anger rising again. "He doesn't trust anyone, okay? Not fully. He used me to get into Phoenix, but he wasn't about to give me an invite to his clubhouse."

The junior investigator softened her tone. "What about communications? How does he contact you?"

Bill's shoulders sagged. "Encrypted messages. He uses a custom app, something he coded himself. No phone calls, no face-to-face. He deletes everything on his end after each exchange."

The lead investigator exchanged a glance with her junior colleague, then leaned in closer. "If you're lying, Billif you're holding anything back we'll know. And when we do, there won't be another chance to save yourself."

Bill's voice broke slightly as he responded, "That's all I know. I swear. If I knew more, I'd tell you."

The junior investigator folded her arms, her voice thoughtful. "We'll see. For now, sit tight. You might not know where Sentinel is, but you've given us enough to start looking."

As the investigators rose to leave, Bill slumped back in his chair, the defiance drained from him. He stared at the mirrored glass, knowing his part in the scheme was far from over, even as his grip on the situation unraveled.

Back in the command room, the team continued their relentless work. Jason and Sarah were focused on narrowing down Sentinel's potential location using utility records and honeypot data. The atmosphere was tense but electric; each new clue brought them closer to their target.

Randon's phone buzzed on the console, interrupting the flow of activity. He glanced at the screen and answered quickly, stepping aside. "Randon here."

The lead investigator's voice came through, sharp and direct. "We just finished questioning Bill. He's given us three potential locations for Sentinel's base: near the old power plant, the abandoned trucking yard, and somewhere along the river."

Randon pulled up the team's map of the area, nodding. "That tracks with some of what we've already flagged. Anything else?"

There was a pause on the other end before the investigator continued, her tone shifting. "One more thing. We know who Sentinel is. His name is Max Weller."

Randon froze, his breath catching in his throat. The name hit him like a lightning bolt. He stared blankly at the screen in front of him, his mind racing. *Max? No... it couldn't be.* The investigator's voice droned on, but Randon barely heard her.

"...a former Phoenix employee. Systems architect. Brilliant but volatile. Fired when Phoenix brought in NexTech for security. He's been off the grid ever since."

Randon swallowed hard, his face pale as he glanced over at Jason. Their eyes met, and Jason frowned, catching the strange look on Randon's face. Randon quickly averted his gaze, masking his shock as best he could. "Got it," he said, his voice tight. "Thanks for the update. I'll relay the information to the team."

"Good," the investigator replied. "Local authorities are preparing for a raid. Focus on narrowing down the exact location. Time is critical."

Randon ended the call and took a deep breath, steadying himself before turning back to the team. "All right, listen up. I just got an update from the investigators. Bill's given us three possible locations for Sentinel's base: near the old power plant, the abandoned trucking yard, and somewhere along the river."

Jason leaned forward, his eyes narrowing. "Do we have anything that can pinpoint which one it is?"

Randon avoided Jason's gaze, his voice steady but distant. "Not yet. Let's keep cross-referencing utility records, honeypot logs, and Sarah's OSINT data."

Sarah, oblivious to Randon's internal turmoil, chimed in confidently. "On it. Filtering for power usage spikes and matching them with the locations the investigators mentioned."

Jason nodded but didn't miss the tension radiating from Randon. "Randon, you okay?"

"Fine," Randon said quickly, too quickly. He busied himself with his console, avoiding further questions.

Minutes passed before Sarah exclaimed, "Got it! Utility records show a massive power spike near the power plant three days ago. Combine that with the social media post about the black van, and that's our strongest lead."

Randon snapped back to the task at hand, phoning the information to the investigator. "Focus the raid on the power plant location. It's the most consistent with our findings."

"Copy that," the investigator replied. "The task force is moving in. Stand by for updates."

As Randon hung up, he turned back to the team. "They're deploying now. If we're right, this could be the break we've been waiting for."

Jason nodded, but his eyes lingered on Randon. Something

was off, and Jason could feel it.

The minutes stretched on, the hum of the command room filling the silence. Finally, Randon turned to Jason, his voice low and almost reluctant. "Jason... there's something I need to tell you."

Jason raised an eyebrow. "What is it?"

Randon hesitated, his jaw tightening. Then, almost in a whisper, he said, "Sentinel... it's Max. Max Weller."

Jason froze, his mind reeling. "Max?" he echoed, his voice barely audible.

Randon gave him a grave look, his expression heavy with the weight of the revelation. "Yeah. Our Max. This is why I called you on this. I suspected it was him a while ago, but without proof, I couldn't say anything. Not to Phoenix. Not to anyone."

Jason stared at him, his mind racing through memorieslong nights tinkering with computers, sharing jokes, dreaming of the future. "And you didn't think to tell me?"

Randon's face tightened with guilt. "I couldn't. Not without risking everything. If I'd been wrong, it would have blown up in my face, and now... now it's too real. He's turned everything we taught him into this."

Jason leaned back, his stomach churning. "Max," he repeated, the name feeling foreign now. "How the hell did we miss this?"

Randon ran a hand through his hair, his voice strained. "I don't know. But I do know this: if Max is Sentinel, then this just got a lot more personal. He knows us, Jason, how we think, how we work. He's not just another hacker. He's one of us, and he's using that against us."

"Randon!?" Karen loudly shouted. "What about Danny!? And Steve???"

"Oh no worries about them, I made sure they had been released right after we got a confession from Bill. They are on their way home, neither wanted to come back just yet."

Chapter 9 - A Bright Future

The command room buzzed with quiet intensity as Sentinel's probes continued, each attempt growing more desperate. Karen sat at the central console, her focus sharp as she countered his every move. Jason stood nearby, his arms crossed, his gaze fixed on the scrolling logs.

The chime of Randon's phone broke the rhythm. He glanced at the notification, then sighed. "Im being called to the stakeholders' meeting. They want a full update and plans for moving forward Jason, I want you to go with me."

Jason gave a small nod. Randon turned to Karen. "You're in charge here. Sentinel's still poking around, but he's running out of options."

Karen smirked, her hands never leaving the keyboard. "Don't worry. I've got him."

Randon and Jason exchanged a glance, then left the command room. The corridor to the conference room felt longer than usual, every step adding to the weight of what they knew and what they suspected was still hidden.

The conference room was dim, its atmosphere heavy with secrecy. Shadowy figures, the stakeholders, occupied the far end of the table, their faces half-hidden. Phoenix representatives sat to the right, their postures rigid, while two government liaisons sat to the left, their expressions a mix of unease and confusion.

Jason and Randon entered quietly, taking seats near the middle. The sharp-featured lead Phoenix representative rose to address the room, her voice calm but clipped.

"We've convened to discuss the recent incident," she began. "Our systems were targeted by a sophisticated adversary. While the breach was contained, significant information was exfiltrated. This creates... operational challenges."

Randon straightened in his seat, prepared to deliver his briefing. "The attack was orchestrated by an individual we've identified as Sentinel. Exploiting insider access, he infiltrated our systems and accessed classified data. Thanks to counter-offensive measures, we neutralized his operation and tracked him to his location."

One of the stakeholders leaned forward slightly, his voice smooth and almost playful. "Neutralized, you say? And the malware you deployed was your idea, Jason?"

Jason glanced up but said nothing, his face impassive. The stakeholder chuckled. "Clever. Diabolical, even. I like it. Imagine what someone like him could do against the competition." He cast a sly grin at his colleagues.

Another stakeholder smirked faintly, while the lead Phoenix representative cleared her throat sharply, cutting the moment short. "Our focus is on securing operations, not expanding capabilities," she said coldly, her gaze silencing any dissent.

The lead Phoenix representative turned to the government liaisons. "This breach has compromised several sensitive operations. As a result, certain shipments will need to be delayed."

One liaison stiffened, clearing his throat nervously. "Delayed? With all due respect, these shipments are critical. A delay could"

The sharp-featured woman cut him off. "We are well aware

of the implications. However, until this matter is resolved, we cannot proceed. Your job, gentlemen, is to ensure local authorities are applying maximum pressure to apprehend Sentinel and retrieve his equipment."

The second liaison shifted uncomfortably. "We've already escalated requests to the task force"

"Then escalate them further," one of the stakeholders interrupted, his voice low and icy. "We need Sentinel's rig. All of it. By any means necessary."

The room fell silent, the weight of the demand hanging in the air.

The tactical team moved silently through the darkened industrial zone, their boots crunching softly against the gravel. The target warehouse loomed ahead, its exterior plain and unassuming. Inside, the hum of equipment and the rhythmic clicking of a keyboard betrayed its occupant. The team leader raised a fist, signaling the group to halt just outside the steel door.

Inside, a man sat at a cluttered workstation surrounded by tangled wires, stacks of notebooks, and glowing monitors. He worked steadily, his fingers moving with practiced speed as he typed. His expression was calm, even content, as though the task at hand were routine. No sweat, no trembling, just quiet focus as he glanced occasionally at the clock on one of his screens.

The tactical leader gave a sharp nod. A breaching charge was placed against the door, and in one coordinated motion, the team exploded inside, their voices cutting through the stillness. "Police! Hands in the air!"

The man paused mid-gesture, his head tilting toward the commotion with mild interest. Turning in his chair, he slowly raised his hands, smiling as if greeting an old friend. "Oh hey, guys. You could've just knocked, you know. I'd have opened the door."

"Step away from the computer! Now!" one of the officers barked, their weapons trained on him.

"Sure, sure," he replied, standing up leisurely. "But can you at least save my game? It took me ages to get to this level."

The officers exchanged glances, unsure whether to be irritated or bemused. "Keep your hands where we can see them," one ordered as they moved in to secure him.

As they zip-tied his wrists, the man grinned. "You know, I've got this amazing Raspberry Pi setup back there. Bet you guys haven't seen one like it. Retro gaming machine, plus it runs my smart lights. Pretty cool, huh?"

One of the younger officers couldn't help but chime in. "What OS are you running on it?"

"Oh, just your classic RetroPie with some custom scripts. It's awesome for emulator support. Are you into retro stuff?"

"Yeah, man. I've got a setup at home. Super Nintendo's my jam."

"Nice! Gotta love the classics." The man's smile widened as they led him toward the center of the room. "You should see the setup I've got for arcade games. One joystick, and you're Pac-Man royalty."

"Enough!" the team leader snapped, breaking the moment. "Get him outside."

The man gave an exaggerated shrug, still smiling. "Guess

the tour's over. But hey, check the notebooks they've got great doodles in the margins."

As they escorted him to the waiting van, he looked back at the officers gathering evidence and chuckled. "Careful with the green notebook. That one's got my grandma's secret cookie recipe."

Back inside, the officers worked to dismantle the operation. Monitors, servers, and routers were carefully packed into evidence crates. Stacks of handwritten notebooks, filled with diagrams, notes, and sketches, were cataloged and bagged.

One officer flipped through a page, spotting an intricate doodle of a robot holding a coffee mug. "This guy's weird," he muttered.

The team leader rolled his eyes. "Weird or not, make sure we grab everything."

Outside, as they loaded the man into the police van, one of the younger officers muttered, "I kinda wanna see that retro setup."

The man winked. "You bring me some tacos during questioning, and maybe I'll let you in on the build specs."

The officer stifled a laugh as the van doors closed, cutting off the man's cheerful banter. As the van pulled away, the tactical team gathered their gear, leaving the darkened warehouse behind.

Back in the conference room, Randon's phone buzzed as the meeting continued. He glanced down at the notification: *Sentinel apprehended.* He stayed silent, his face betraying no reaction. Moments later, other phones buzzed across the room. The government liaisons exchanged hurried whispers, while the Phoenix representatives and stakeholders remained eerily calm.

"Well," one stakeholder murmured, his tone almost amused. "That's one problem solved."

The lead Phoenix representative's gaze swept the room. "The situation is contained. For now. But the recovery of all exfiltrated data remains our top priority."

Karen's phone buzzed with the same notification. She allowed herself a small smile before turning back to the monitor. "Gotcha," she muttered, watching as Sentinel's activity finally ceased.

As the meeting broke up, Jason and Randon walked back toward the command room in silence. Randon finally spoke, his voice low. "They're hiding something. You heard them."

Jason's jaw tightened. "Yeah. And now we know where to look."

Chapter 10 Epilogue - A New Beginning

The interrogation room buzzed with quiet tension as the mystery man sat casually at the metal table, his hands cuffed in front of him. He leaned back in his chair, a faint smile playing on his lips, as if this was all some elaborate misunderstanding.

Across from him, two interrogators leaned forward, their faces etched with frustration. The lead investigator slapped a folder onto the table. "We've got you dead to rights. The equipment, the notebooks, the logs. You're Sentinel, and you're not walking out of here until we get answers."

The man arched an eyebrow, unfazed. "Sentinel? That's a cool name, but no, sorry. Not me. I'm more of a digital janitor, you know? Cleaning up messes."

The junior investigator frowned. "Cleaning up? Is that what you call wiping drives and hiding evidence? Who hired you?"

The man grinned. "Wouldn't you like to know? But hey, you're the professionals, don't you have ways to figure that out? Maybe check your logs or whatever?"

The lead investigator's jaw tightened. "You're awfully smug for someone in your position."

"Smug? Nah. I just figure we might as well enjoy the conversation. It's not every day I get to chat with people who care this much about my work." He glanced at the one-way mirror and waved. "Hi, by the way. Are you guys doing okay back there?"

Meanwhile, outside the interrogation room, Jason and Randon stood watching through the one-way glass. Jason's arms were crossed, his expression dark. "That's not him," he muttered. "This guy isn't Sentinel."

Randon nodded, his phone already in his hand. "Yeah, I know. I've been piecing it together since the arrest. He doesn't match Max's MOtoo relaxed, too cooperative."

"So what do we do?" Jason asked, his voice low.

Randon tapped out a quick message to the lead investigator, explaining the mix-up. "I'm letting them know now. This isn't the guy. Max set this whole thing up, probably paid him off to wipe the gear and play along."

Jason shook his head, the weight of the realization settling over him. "Max is still out there, isn't he?"

"Yeah," Randon replied, his tone grim. "And he's laughing at us right now."

Back in the interrogation room, the investigators hadn't gotten the message yet. The lead investigator leaned forward, his tone sharp. "If you're not Sentinel, then why were you caught with his equipment? The logs, the servers, the notebooks; it all points to you."

The man shrugged nonchalantly. "Look, I was just doing a gig. Someone needed a system cleaned up, I'm good at cleaning. End of story." He tilted his head, his smile widening. "But hey, since we're here, want me to recommend a good antivirus? You'd be amazed how many people still fall for phishing scams."

The junior investigator blinked, momentarily caught off guard. "Antivirus? Are you serious right now?"

"Absolutely. Gotta start with the basics, right? Prevention is key." He gestured toward the folder. "You guys seem thorough. Ever hear of sandboxing? It's a game-changer."

The lead investigator slammed his hand on the table. "Enough! This isn't a tech support seminar!"

The man shrugged again, utterly unbothered. "Your loss. I was about to give you a great tip on securing IoT devices."

Jason and Randon returned to the command room, the tension following them like a shadow. Sarah looked up from her workstation. "What's the word? Did they get anything out of him?"

Jason shook his head. "They're wasting their time. That guy's not Sentinel."

Karen frowned, glancing at the live feed of the interrogation. "Then who is he?"

"Some hired cleaner," Randon said. "Max paid him off to wipe the evidence and buy himself time."

Jason leaned on the console, his gaze distant. "Max is still out there. And now we're back to square one."

As the team worked to clean up the digital mess Sentinel had left behind, Randon's phone buzzed with a news alert. He glanced at it, his jaw tightening as he read the headline: *NexTech Takes Down Notorious Hacker in Landmark Operation.*

Jason noticed the look on Randon's face. "What now?"

Randon held up the phone, the headline glaringly bold. Jason sighed, shaking his head. "Figures. They sweep in, claim credit, and get the glory."

"They were watching," Steve said, not even looking up from his screen. "Of course they'd spin it their way."

Karen rolled her eyes. "Classic NexTech. All flash, no substance."

Jason smirked faintly, but his eyes remained hard. "Let them have their story. We know the truth."

As the night stretched on, the team continued their work, patching vulnerabilities and shoring up defenses. The command room buzzed with activity, but beneath it all, a quiet determination had taken hold.

Jason and Randon sat in a corner, their voices low. "Do you think we'll see him again?" Jason asked.

Randon nodded slowly. "Yeah. Max isn't done. He'll show up again, one way or another."

Jason exhaled, his gaze steady. "Next time, we'll be ready. Either he's on our side, or he's behind bars."

Randon gave a faint smile. "Agreed. But until then, let's focus on what we can control. There's a lot of work to do."

Jason leaned back, a glint of resolve in his eyes. "We'll get it done. One way or another."

A week later, Jason sat in his garage, the scent of motor oil and aged metal hanging in the air. The soft hum of a desk fan filled the quiet as he tinkered with an old circuit board, his hands moving automatically while his mind wandered. The phone on his workbench buzzed, pulling him from his thoughts. The caller ID read: *NexTech HR.*

Jason sighed and answered. The voice on the other end was polished, professional, and enthusiastic. The offer was laid out with precision: a high-ranking position, a generous salary, access to cutting-edge projects, and the chance to work with some of the brightest minds in cybersecurity. It was everything Jason had once dreamed of, or so he thought. But now, it feels hollow.

"Thank you for the offer," Jason said after the pitch ended. "But I'm going to have to decline."

There was a moment of stunned silence on the other end. "Are you sure, Mr. Cole? This is a rare opportunity"

"I'm sure," Jason interrupted, his voice firm. "It's just not the right fit for me."

After ending the call, Jason leaned back in his chair, staring at the ceiling. The idea of joining a bureaucratic giant like NexTech had no appeal. He wanted something real, something with purpose. An idea began to form, and a grin slowly spread across his face.

Later that evening, Jason met with Randon at their usual spot, a quiet diner just outside the city. Over steaming cups of coffee, Jason shared his decision.

"NexTech called," Jason began, stirring his coffee absently. "Offered me a cushy job."

Randon raised an eyebrow. "And you said no?"

Jason nodded, the grin still on his face. "Didn't even hesitate."

Randon leaned back, a knowing smile spreading across his face. "So, what's next?"

Jason's eyes gleamed with excitement. "We start our own firm. No bureaucracy, no politics, just real cybersecurity work. We take on the threats no one else will touch."

"You're serious?" Randon asked, though the spark in his eyes suggested he already knew the answer.

"Dead serious," Jason replied. "And I think we've got a few people who'd join us."

Over the next few weeks, the pieces began to fall into place. Jason and Randon worked late nights drafting plans, sketching ideas on whiteboards, and debating their firm's mission. They agreed on one thing: their focus would be on tackling threats that others ignored or didn't understand, with a commitment to staying independent and ethical.

Their first recruit was Sarah. She was impressed by Jason's leadership during the crisis and his willingness to take bold risks. "I'm in," she said without hesitation. "But I'm keeping my role at NexTech. Someone needs to keep an eye on those guys."

"Good," Jason replied with a grin. "We could use someone on the inside."

Next came Steve. He had spent weeks rebuilding his reputation after being falsely accused, and the chance to join something meaningful was exactly what he needed. "I want in," Steve said, his voice steady with determination. "I need this, for me and for everyone who believes in me."

Karen was next. Her loyalty to Phoenix was gone, but she saw the value in staying embedded. "I'll help from the inside," she said. "Phoenix has too many secrets. If we're going to expose them, we need someone there."

One by one, others from the command room team joined as well, each bringing unique skills and perspectives. They were building something extraordinary, not just a firm but a family united by purpose.

On their last night in the Phoenix command room, the group gathered for one final task: securing the network against future attacks. The room buzzed with energy as they worked, each person focused on their role. Laughter occasionally broke the tension, and for the first time in weeks, the atmosphere felt light.

Jason stood at the center, watching his team with pride. These were the people he trusted, the ones who had been in the trenches with him. For the first time in a long while, he felt hopeful. The world was full of threats, but now, they had the means to fight back.

The monitors blinked off one by one as the final tasks were completed. The team exchanged glances, a quiet sense of accomplishment settling over them.

Randon walked over to Jason, his hands in his pockets. "This is just the beginning," he said, his voice steady.

Jason nodded, a faint smile playing on his lips. "Let's make it count."

The End

Cyber Vocabulary

A

- Access Control: Mechanisms that limit access to resources based on user permissions.
- Antivirus Software: Programs designed to detect, prevent, and remove malware.
- Authentication: The process of verifying the identity of a user or system.
- Authorization: The process of determining if a user has permission to access a resource.

B

- Backup: A copy of data stored separately to recover from loss or corruption.
- Breach: An incident where unauthorized access to data occurs.
- Botnet: A network of compromised computers controlled by a single attacker.

C

- Cloud Security: Measures taken to protect data in cloud computing environments.
- Cryptography: The practice of securing information by converting it into an unreadable format.

D

- DDoS Attack: A Distributed Denial of Service attack aimed at overwhelming a target.
- Data Breach Notification: A legal requirement to inform individuals of compromised data.

- Data Loss Prevention (DLP): Strategies to ensure sensitive data is not lost or misused.
- Encryption: The process of converting plaintext into ciphertext to protect data.
- Endpoint Security: Protection measures for devices like laptops and smartphones.

F

- Firewall: A security device or software that monitors and controls network traffic.
- Forensics: The process of collecting and analyzing data to investigate cyber incidents.

H

- Hacker: An individual who exploits vulnerabilities in systems.
- Incident: Any event that compromises the confidentiality, integrity, or availability of information.
- Incident Response: Procedures for detecting and responding to cybersecurity incidents.
- Insider Threat: Security risks posed by individuals within an organization.
- Intrusion Detection System (IDS): Monitors network traffic for suspicious activity.

M

- Malware: Malicious software designed to harm or exploit devices.
- Multi-Factor Authentication (MFA): Requires two or more forms of verification to access resources.

N

- Network Security: Measures to protect the integrity and usability of a network.
- Third-Party Risk: Security threats posed by vendors or partners with access to data.

O

- Cyber Hygiene: Best practices for maintaining the security of IT systems.
- GDPR (General Data Protection Regulation): Regulation on data protection and privacy in the EU.

P

- Patch Management: Managing updates to software and systems to fix vulnerabilities.
- Phishing: A social engineering attack to trick users into providing sensitive information.
- Privilege Escalation: Gaining elevated access to resources that are normally protected.
- Public Key Infrastructure (PKI): A framework for managing digital certificates and encryption.

R

- Ransomware: Malware that encrypts files and demands payment for decryption.
- Red Team/Blue Team: Simulated attacks and defenses to test security.
- Rootkit: Tools used to gain unauthorized access while hiding their presence.

S

- Sandboxing: Running applications in a controlled environment for testing.
- Security Audit: Evaluating an organization's security policies and controls.
- Security Policy: A formal document outlining an organization's security approach.
- Security Token: A device or digital key for accessing systems.
- Session Hijacking: Taking control of a user session after authentication.
- Social Engineering: Manipulating individuals into divulging confidential information.
- Spoofing: Disguising a communication to appear as from a trusted source.
- Spyware: Software that secretly monitors and collects user data.

T

- Threat Intelligence: Information to understand potential threats to systems.
- Vulnerability: A weakness in a system that can be exploited.
- VPN (Virtual Private Network): Creates a secure connection over the internet.
- Web Application Firewall (WAF): Protects web applications by filtering HTTP traffic.
- Whaling: A phishing attack targeting high-profile individuals.
- Zero-Day Exploit: An attack that occurs on the same day a vulnerability is discovered.

U

- User Education: Training programs to educate users about cybersecurity best practices.

Types of Cyber attacks

1. Phishing

Description: Phishing attacks involve fraudulent emails or messages that appear to come from legitimate sources. The goal is to deceive users into providing sensitive information, such as usernames, passwords, or credit card numbers.
Example: An email that looks like it's from a bank, asking the recipient to verify their account by clicking a link.

2. Spear Phishing

Description: Unlike general phishing, spear phishing targets specific individuals or organizations. Attackers often gather personal information to craft convincing messages.
Example: An attacker posing as a colleague to request sensitive data from an employee.

3. Ransomware

Description: Ransomware is malicious software that encrypts a victim's files or locks them out of their system, demanding payment (usually in cryptocurrency) to restore access.
Example: The WannaCry attack that affected thousands of organizations worldwide, demanding ransom payments in Bitcoin.

4. Malware

Description: Malware is a broad category of malicious software designed to harm, exploit, or otherwise compromise devices and networks. It includes viruses, worms, trojans, and spyware.
Example: A trojan horse that appears to be a legitimate application but secretly installs harmful software.

5. DDoS Attack (Distributed Denial of Service)

Description: DDoS attacks flood a target's servers with excessive traffic, rendering them unable to respond to legitimate requests. This can lead to downtime and service disruption.
Example: An attack that overwhelms an online service like a gaming platform, making it inaccessible to users.

6. SQL Injection

Description: SQL injection exploits vulnerabilities in a web application's database layer by injecting malicious SQL queries. This can allow attackers to manipulate or access sensitive data.
Example: A poorly designed login form that allows attackers to bypass authentication by entering SQL code.

7. Cross-Site Scripting (XSS)

Description: XSS attacks involve injecting malicious scripts into web pages that are viewed by users. This can lead to unauthorized actions being performed on behalf of the user.

Example: An attacker injecting a script into a comment section, which then executes when other users view the comment.

8. Man-in-the-Middle (MitM)

Description: MitM attacks occur when an attacker secretly intercepts and relays communications between two parties. This allows the attacker to eavesdrop or alter the messages.
Example: An attacker intercepting data transmitted over an unsecured Wi-Fi network.

9. Credential Stuffing

Description: This attack uses stolen username and password pairs from one breach to access accounts on different services, exploiting users who reuse passwords.
Example: An attacker uses credentials from a leaked database to gain access to a victim's email account.

10. Zero-Day Exploit

Description: A zero-day exploit targets vulnerabilities in software that are unknown to the vendor. Attackers take advantage of these vulnerabilities before a patch is released.
Example: An exploit that targets a flaw in popular software shortly after its discovery by hackers.

11. Insider Threat

Description: Insider threats involve employees or contractors who misuse their access to compromise the organization's security, either intentionally or unintentionally.
Example: An employee leaking sensitive information to a competitor or inadvertently exposing data through negligence.

12. Advanced Persistent Threats (APTs)

Description: APTs are prolonged and targeted attacks where an intruder gains access to a network and remains undetected for an extended period, often to steal data.
Example: A state-sponsored attack that infiltrates a government network to exfiltrate sensitive information over time.

13. Drive-By Download

Description: This attack occurs when a user unknowingly downloads malicious software while visiting a compromised website. No user interaction is needed.
Example: Visiting a site that hosts malicious ads that automatically download malware onto the user's device.

14. IoT Attacks

Description: IoT attacks target vulnerabilities in Internet of Things devices, which often lack robust security measures, allowing attackers to exploit them.
Example: Hacking a smart home device to gain access to a home network.

15. Business Email Compromise (BEC)

Description: BEC attacks involve spoofing a legitimate business email account to trick employees into wiring money or sharing sensitive information.
Example: An attacker impersonating a CEO to instruct an employee to transfer funds to a fraudulent account.

16. Worms

Description: Worms are self-replicating malware that spread across networks without needing a host file or user action. They can exploit vulnerabilities to propagate.
Example: The Conficker worm that infected millions of computers by exploiting security flaws.

17. Botnets

Description: A botnet is a network of infected devices controlled by an attacker, often used to perform large-scale attacks like DDoS or send spam.
Example: The Mirai botnet, which leveraged IoT devices to launch a massive DDoS attack.

18. DNS Spoofing

Description: DNS spoofing involves corrupting the DNS cache to redirect users from legitimate sites to malicious ones, often for phishing or malware distribution.
Example: Redirecting users from a bank's website to a fake site designed to steal login credentials.

19. Physical Attacks

Description: Physical attacks involve gaining unauthorized physical access to systems or devices to compromise security, steal data, or install malware.
Example: An attacker breaking into an office to steal a server or access sensitive information directly.

20. Social Engineering

Description: Social engineering exploits human psychology to manipulate individuals into divulging confidential information or performing actions that compromise security.
Example: An attacker impersonating IT support to convince an employee to share their login credentials.

Cybersecurity Job Types

1. Security Analyst

Description: Security analysts are responsible for monitoring an organization's IT infrastructure for security threats. They analyze security incidents, manage security tools, and respond to alerts to mitigate risks.
Key Responsibilities:

- Monitor network traffic and security alerts.
- Conduct vulnerability assessments.
- Create reports on security incidents and suggest improvements.

2. Security Engineer

Description: Security engineers design and implement security systems to protect an organization's infrastructure. They work on securing hardware, software, and networks.
Key Responsibilities:

- Develop security architectures and frameworks.
- Implement security controls and countermeasures.
- Test and evaluate security products and systems.

3. Penetration Tester (Ethical Hacker)

Description: Penetration testers simulate cyber attacks to identify vulnerabilities in systems, networks, and applications. They provide insights on how to improve

security.
Key Responsibilities:

- Conduct penetration tests and vulnerability assessments.
- Document findings and provide recommendations.
- Collaborate with development teams to address vulnerabilities.

4. Security Consultant

Description: Security consultants provide expert advice to organizations on improving their security posture. They assess risks and help develop security strategies tailored to the organization.
Key Responsibilities:

- Perform security assessments and audits.
- Develop security policies and procedures.
- Advise on compliance with regulations and standards.

5. Incident Response Specialist

Description: Incident response specialists manage and respond to security incidents. They investigate breaches, contain damage, and implement recovery plans.
Key Responsibilities:

- Develop and maintain incident response plans.
- Investigate security breaches and document findings.
- Coordinate recovery efforts and post-incident analysis.

6. Network Security Administrator

Description: Network security administrators manage and secure an organization's network infrastructure. They ensure that network access is secure and monitor for unauthorized activities.

Key Responsibilities:

- Configure and maintain firewalls, routers, and VPNs.
- Monitor network traffic for anomalies.
- Conduct regular security audits and assessments.

7. Cybersecurity Architect

Description: Cybersecurity architects design the overall security framework for an organization. They develop strategies to safeguard systems and ensure compliance with security standards.

Key Responsibilities:

- Create security models and policies.
- Evaluate and select security technologies.
- Collaborate with other IT teams to integrate security into systems.

8. Malware Analyst

Description: Malware analysts study and dissect malicious software to understand its behavior and impact. They help develop defenses against malware.

Key Responsibilities:

- Analyze malware samples in controlled environments.
- Create signatures and indicators of compromise

(IOCs).

- Share findings with security teams to enhance defenses.

9. Threat Intelligence Analyst

Description: Threat intelligence analysts collect and analyze information about potential threats to help organizations anticipate and respond to cyber attacks.
Key Responsibilities:

- Research and analyze threat actors and their tactics.
- Produce intelligence reports and threat assessments.
- Collaborate with incident response teams to provide insights.

10. Compliance Analyst

Description: Compliance analysts ensure that organizations adhere to regulatory requirements and industry standards related to cybersecurity.
Key Responsibilities:

- Conduct audits to assess compliance with security policies.
- Prepare reports for regulatory bodies.
- Develop and implement compliance programs.

11. Security Operations Center (SOC) Analyst

Description: SOC analysts work in a security operations center, monitoring security systems and responding to incidents in real-time.

Key Responsibilities:

- Monitor alerts from security information and event management (SIEM) systems.
- Investigate security incidents and escalate as necessary.
- Maintain documentation of incidents and responses.

12. Cloud Security Specialist

Description: Cloud security specialists focus on securing cloud environments and ensuring that data stored in the cloud is protected.

Key Responsibilities:

- Implement security controls for cloud services.
- Assess risks associated with cloud deployments.
- Monitor cloud activity for unauthorized access.

13. Chief Information Security Officer (CISO)

Description: The CISO is responsible for an organization's overall information security strategy, ensuring that security practices align with business goals.

Key Responsibilities:

- Develop and implement security policies and procedures.
- Manage security teams and budgets.
- Report to executive leadership on security risks and initiatives.

14. Forensics Analyst

Description: Forensics analysts investigate cyber crimes and security incidents, collecting and analyzing digital evidence to understand what happened.

Key Responsibilities:

- Perform forensic examinations on compromised systems.
- Document findings and prepare reports for legal proceedings.
- Work with law enforcement if needed.

15. DevSecOps Engineer

Description: DevSecOps engineers integrate security practices into the software development lifecycle, ensuring that applications are secure from the start.

Key Responsibilities:

- Collaborate with development teams to implement security measures.
- Automate security testing and monitoring.
- Educate teams on secure coding practices.

16. Identity and Access Management (IAM) Specialist

Description: IAM specialists manage user identities and access controls to ensure that only authorized individuals have access to sensitive information.

Key Responsibilities:

- Implement IAM policies and procedures.
- Manage user roles and permissions.
- Conduct audits to ensure compliance with access policies.

17. Risk Manager

Description: Risk managers identify and assess cybersecurity risks within an organization, developing strategies to mitigate those risks.
Key Responsibilities:
- Conduct risk assessments and vulnerability analyses.
- Develop risk management policies and procedures.
- Communicate risks to stakeholders and executive leadership.

18. Application Security Engineer

Description: Application security engineers focus on securing software applications throughout their development lifecycle, identifying and addressing vulnerabilities.
Key Responsibilities:
- Conduct security reviews and assessments of applications.
- Collaborate with developers to implement secure coding practices.
- Test applications for vulnerabilities and provide remediation guidance.

19. Information Security Manager

Description: Information security managers oversee an organization's information security program, ensuring compliance with policies and regulations.

Key Responsibilities:

- Develop and enforce security policies and procedures.
- Manage security awareness training for employees.
- Coordinate incident response efforts.

20. Cybersecurity Trainer/Educator

Description: Cybersecurity trainers provide education and training on cybersecurity best practices to employees, helping to foster a culture of security awareness.

Key Responsibilities:

- Develop training materials and programs.
- Conduct workshops and training sessions.
- Evaluate the effectiveness of training initiatives.